PUDDLE QUESTIONS for Science

GRADE 6

Performance Assessment Investigations

Heather McDonald
Joan Westley

Creative Publications

Writers: Heather McDonald, Nancy Tune, Joan Westley
Editors: Judith Brand, Sarah Le Forge, Mary Scott Martinson, and Nancy Tune
Spanish Translation: OSO Publishing Services
Production Coordinator: Joe Shines
Design and Production: London Road Design, Palo Alto, CA
Cover Art: Jim M'Guinness
Illustrations: Jane McCreary, Jim M'Guinness

With special thanks to Cindy Reak.

1300 Villa Street
Mountain View, California 94041-1197

ISBN: 1-56107-846-8

2 3 4 5 6 7 8 9 10 9 8 7 6

Table of Contents

Acknowledgments

About seventy teachers in twenty-nine schools in five states field tested the problems in this series with approximately two thousand students. Heartfelt thanks to every one of you—especially the students, whose responses we treasure.

Classroom Coordinators: Julia Alexander, Kelli Bergren, Chris Casey, Roberta Cole, Shirley Danklefs, Diana Dickinson, Jodie Dillman, Joan Elder, Gerry Elgarten, Beth Farina, Sandy Jones, Dr. Vi Lien, Tom Lyons, Barbara Mohs, Nelda Montejano, Dr. Anne Papakonstantinou, Delia Sanchez, Gen Sapirstein, Lyn Ungrodt, Avery Walker, Laurie Waring

Participating Schools:

California
Fair (J. Wilbur), San Jose
Hillview, Menlo Park
Jean Farb, San Diego
Jordan, Palo Alto
Mid-Peninsula Jewish Community, Palo Alto
Monroe, Campbell
Mulholland, Van Nuys
Neal Dow, Chico
Ohlone, Palo Alto
Paradise, Paradise
Ponderosa, Paradise
Santa Rita, Los Altos
Warwick, Fremont
Woodland, Menlo Park

Florida
Bear Lake, Apopka
English Estates, Fern Park
Forest City, Altamont Springs
Heathrow, Lake Mary
Lake Orienta, Altamont Springs
Partin, Oviedo
Stenstrom, Oviedo

Oregon
Beaver Acres, Aloha
Sexton Mountain, Beaverton

Texas
Athens, San Antonio
HISD/Rice K-8, Houston
Hutchins, San Antonio
Palo Alto, San Antonio

Wisconsin
Wingra, Madison

What Are Puddle Questions™?

The Puddle Questions project grew out of an experience with a classroom of K–2 students several years ago. We asked these students the deceptively simple question: "How would you go about measuring a puddle?"

How students answered this question was revealing in a number of ways. Because the question was so open-ended, it put the responsibility for thinking into the hands of the students. It enabled us to assess how individual students were able to think through a complex investigation, plan an approach, use tools and techniques, draw conclusions, and communicate their thinking.

The original puddle question led to the development of many other thought-provoking math investigations, which were piloted in classrooms across the country. The questions were compiled into a 1–8 series, **Puddle Questions: Assessing Mathematical Thinking.**

With the success of this series, we turned our attention to how open-ended, rich questions could be used in science assessment. In **Puddle Questions for Science,** *we wanted to find out how students work through a complex investigation without the structure or hand holding that typifies much of science education today, where each step of an investigation is mapped out for the student, from the equipment needed to the way results should be displayed.*

In contrast, we wanted to see how students themselves handle the full range of tasks a scientist performs: making careful observations, gathering data, conducting research, designing experiments, and interpreting results. We wanted to assess science processes rather than specific facts or knowledge. While we wanted the questions to be challenging, we also wanted the investigations to be approachable by students with the full range of ability levels and diverse backgrounds that characterize our classrooms today.

As we piloted **Puddle Questions for Science,** *we found that students (and their teachers) often were unsure initially that they could perform well on these assessment tasks. But when responses came back to us, we delighted in the variety of unique ways students had found to approach the investigations. We are proud to share their work with you in this book.*

Sincerely,

Joan Westley
Heather McDonald

Presenting the Investigations

The Teacher's Role

With *Puddle Questions for Science,* as with open-ended assessment in general, the teacher acts as a facilitator. Teachers should hand out the student pages and introduce the investigation briefly before letting the students begin work. (Student pages in both English and Spanish are provided on pages 77–92.) Be sure students understand that there is no one way to approach the tasks. They should also know what they will be evaluated on. For each investigation, assessment criteria are listed in the Presenting the Investigation section of the teaching notes.

Name__________ Date__________

Investigation 4 **Melt an Ice Cube**

Suppose you want an ice cube to melt as fast as possible. What are some things you could do? What would be the fastest way?

Make a list of things you think you could do to make an ice cube melt fast. Design an experiment to test your ideas. Write about what you find out.

Low / Medium / High
Self Assessment

Fecha__________

Investigación 4 **Derrite un cubo de hielo**

Imagínate que quieres que un cubo de hielo se derrita tan rápido como sea posible. ¿Qué puedes hacer para que se derrita? ¿Qué método sería el más rápido?

Haz una lista de las cosas que crees que puedes hacer para que un cubo de hielo se derrita rápidamente. Diseña un experimento para comprobar tus ideas. Luego escribe un informe acerca de lo que hayas descubierto.

Bajo / Regular / Alto
Evaluación propia

While the students work on the investigations, you can use the Prompts for Getting Started questions, posing them either to individuals or to the whole group. This will help remind students of aspects of the question they may not have attended to at first, but that may be more pertinent as they get deeper into the investigation.

Let the students know that these investigations are difficult. They're intended to assess students' abilities to tackle challenging questions and show how they would go about doing what real scientists do. All students should be able to respond in some way, however.

Your most important role once the students get started is to let them work through the investigation themselves. Try not to direct their work into one avenue or another. Give the students the freedom to come up with their own ideas.

If this is your students' first experience with open-ended investigations, they may need extra encouragement. It may take a few investigations before they feel comfortable with the lack of structure in Puddle Questions, especially with the notion of having to choose for themselves what approach to take. Once they have tackled a few of the investigations, their responses will improve considerably.

Materials

Choosing the proper tools is part of the scientific process. Students should have access to any reasonable tools and equipment they need to complete the task. Often a variety of miscellaneous materials are called for so that individual students can select different things to investigate. The important thing is to avoid dictating what materials the students use, or even implying that one material is more appropriate than another. For example, providing polystyrene cups for each student for an investigation might give the false impression that these particular cups must be used for a correct response. A better method is to make a range of materials available. A list of suggested tools and materials is provided in the introduction to each investigation.

Grouping Arrangement

A suggested grouping arrangement is given for each investigation. If students work in pairs or small groups, each student is still responsible for writing up his or her own report.

Time Frame

A suggested time frame is also given for each investigation, although the amount of time needed will vary for individual classrooms and students. Let students work on the investigations as long as they need to. Students who finish early should be asked to review the question and their response to make sure they have done as much with the investigation as they can.

The Role of Observation

In each investigation, we ask the students to write about what they did and what they found out. Because students may not write complete descriptions of what they did, it is important to make careful observations while they are working to get an accurate picture of their performance on the investigation. Your observations can be written on plain note paper, 3" x 5" cards, or on the special Observation Sheets provided on page 95. The questions you should ask yourself as the students work are highlighted with this special "eyeglasses" icon on the Assessing the Work page.

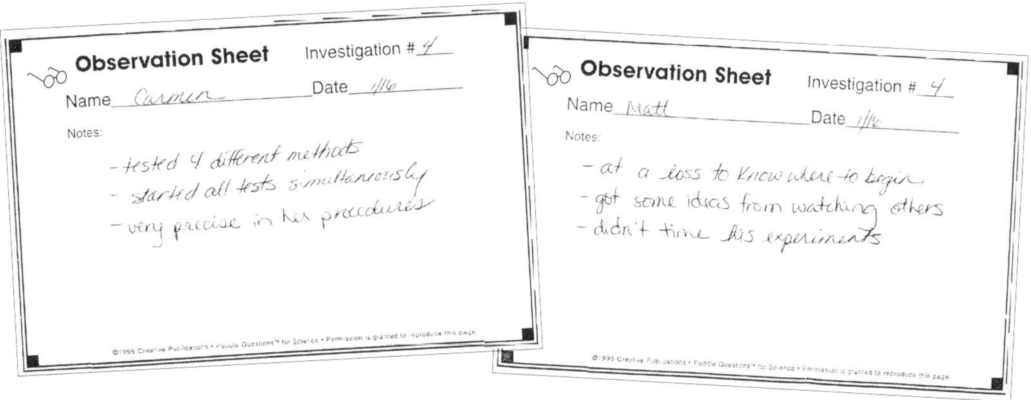

Observation Sheet Investigation # 4

Name Carmen Date 1/16

Notes:

- tested 4 different methods
- started all tests simultaneously
- very precise in her procedures

©1995 Creative Publications • Puzzle Questions™ for Science • Permission is granted to reproduce this page.

Observation Sheet Investigation # 4

Name Matt Date 1/16

Notes:

- at a loss to know where to begin
- got some ideas from watching others
- didn't time his experiments

©1995 Creative Publications • Puzzle Questions™ for Science • Permission is granted to reproduce this page.

The Students' Role

In *Puddle Questions for Science,* we are asking students to take responsibility for choosing their approach, carrying it out, and communicating their ideas. This mirrors the way scientists work. Their tasks are not spelled out for them. Rather, they must think through a question carefully, weigh the merits of different ways to proceed, decide on a plan of action, and carry it out. They are expected to communicate in a way that gives people a clear understanding of what they did and what they found out. Often, they are expected to display data in interesting and easily understandable ways.

Writing reports can be hard for students. Let them use their own invented spellings for words they do not know. Writing in a primary language other than English is also a good idea, if the student would be handicapped writing in English. If student writing is difficult to decipher, you may want the student to read the paper to you so you can understand what is being said. Younger students can also dictate their ideas for you or an aide to do the writing.

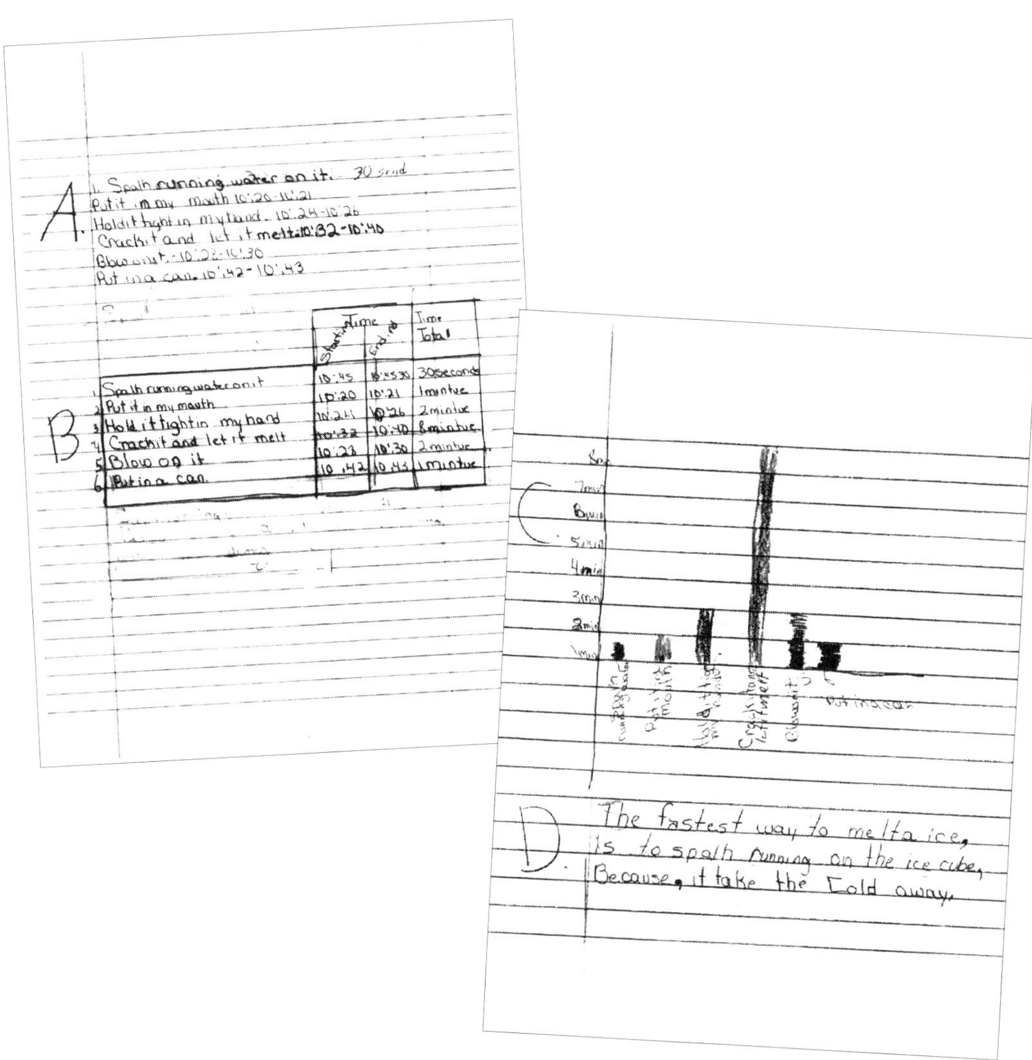

Assessing the Work

Scoring the Responses

We recommend a holistic approach for scoring the responses to the investigations. In a holistic approach, you look at the work globally and give one overall score to the response, rather than giving points for various aspects of the response. The emphasis should be on the use of scientific processes exemplified in the student's work rather than on their understanding of certain scientific concepts or their knowledge of facts. When scoring the responses, you will want to consider the work students do, the reports they write, and any observations you have made as they work.

You can score your students' work using one of the following methods:

- The scoring rubric provided with the investigation. This rubric provides three levels of response to the specific question in the investigation: Low, Medium, and High. You may want to add N/A (no attempt) and INC (incomplete) categories to the rubric.
- The Generalized Scoring Rubric below.
- Your district's own scoring rubric or a scoring rubric of your choice.

Generalized Scoring Rubric

Responses in each category show some of the following characteristics:

Low Response

- Does not apply appropriate scientific processes.
- Fails to address significant aspects of the investigation.
- Lacks clarity and detail.

Medium Response

- Shows an effort to use scientific processes, although they may be somewhat flawed.
- Contains a complete response.
- Communicates fairly clearly with some detail.

High Response

- Applies appropriate scientific processes consistently and thoughtfully.
- Contains a complete and thorough response.
- Communicates clearly with precise language.

Sample Responses

Shown with each investigation are sample responses for each level: High, Medium, and Low. Some responses were gathered at the beginning of the school year, some at the middle, and some at the end. No doubt the same students would have done different work at different times. It is not possible to represent here the full range of responses for these types of investigations. However, studying these samples will give you an idea of the variety of ways students can approach the investigations. The samples may also help you score your class's responses by providing one or two benchmarks for each level. Don't be alarmed, however, if your students' responses do not match the samples. Every classroom is unique. How you score your students' work should be an individual decision, based on their needs and the amount of experience they have had with open-ended investigations.

Portfolios

Students can keep their investigation reports in a special portfolio. This way they can see improvement over the year in their ability to tackle open-ended investigations. These portfolios are also useful for parent conferences. Authentic assessment often helps to show parents what students can and cannot do.

Self Assessment

On the student page is a self-assessment dial. Students are to shade the dial to show the level at which they feel they performed in the investigation. Self-Assessment blackline masters are also available in English and Spanish on pages 93 and 94. For each investigation students can record their performance level and write their reflections on how they did and how they might improve next time. It's interesting to compare students' self-assessment scores to the scores they receive from you for the investigation. You might want to discuss discrepancies between the two should they occur.

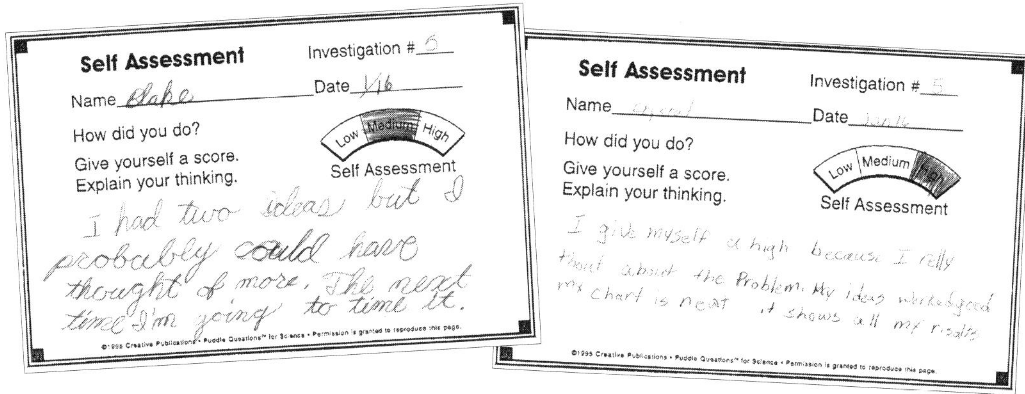

Self Assessment

Investigation # 5

Name Blake

Date 1/16

How did you do?

Give yourself a score.
Explain your thinking.

Low | Medium | High
Self Assessment

I had two ideas but I probably could have thought of more. The next time I'm going to time it.

Self Assessment

Investigation # 5

Name

Date

How did you do?

Give yourself a score.
Explain your thinking.

Low | Medium | High
Self Assessment

I give myself a high because I relly thout about the Problem. My ideas worked good my chart is neat it shows all my rsalts

Extending the Learning

Class Discussion and Sharing

The investigations are intended to be more than just an evaluation of what students can do. They are supposed to be a learning experience. To enhance the learning potential of each investigation, you'll want to follow up with a chance for students to discuss and share the work they did and the variety of ways in which they approached the investigation. Suggestions are given for class discussions for each investigation. The key is to let students explain their own ideas to each other. In doing so, they may (1) realize that they were misdirected in their reasoning, or (2) help others understand how they might have done the investigation differently.

Follow-Up Activity

The follow-up activity described for each investigation is a natural outgrowth of the investigation itself. Its purpose is again to extend the learning experiences inherent in the investigation situation.

Puddle Observations

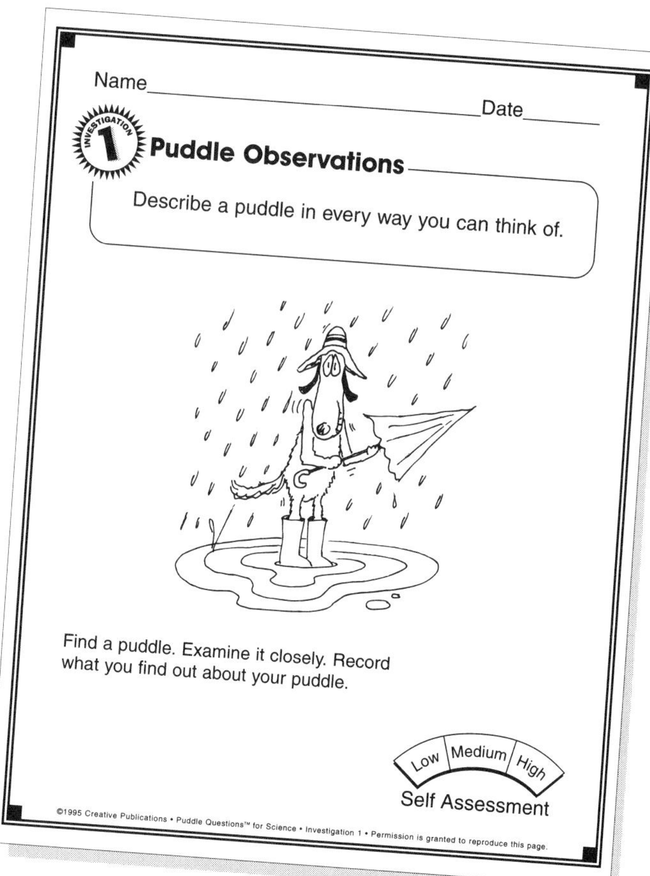
Name
Date
Puddle Observations
Describe a puddle in every way you can think of.

Find a puddle. Examine it closely. Record what you find out about your puddle.

Low Medium High
Self Assessment

Blackline Master in English, page 77
and in Spanish, page 78

One of the most basic yet vital processes scientists use in every aspect of their work is observation. In the spirit of challenging students to become careful observers, we ask them to take a close look at a familiar natural phenomenon: a rain puddle. Puddles were chosen as the focus because they vary widely in consistency, size, shape, and contents (including possibly some organic matter), and thus offer a rich source for observations. But if rain is a rarity in your area, it is possible to substitute other objects in nature. A dead log or a cactus would provide a similar richness. Whatever the focus of the observations, the challenge is to examine it in every way possible.

Science Processes

- Making detailed observations
- Using tools and techniques

Tools and Equipment

- ◆ hand lenses
- ◆ miscellaneous materials (see Presenting the Investigation)
- ◆ blank paper
- ◆ lined writing paper
- ◆ pencils

Grouping Arrangement

Individuals or pairs

Time Frame

1–2 hours

Presenting the Investigation

1. Introduce the puddle investigation on a day when there are standing puddles near the school. Gather the class together and pose the following question: **What do you know about the general skills scientists need to use?** Have the students share their ideas. Discuss with them the fact that scientists need great skill in making observations. **Today we'll put our powers of observation to the test.**
2. Hand out the investigation to the students. **If you examine a puddle closely, what kinds of things do you think you will notice? What are some tools you could take with you to help you make your observations?** Take the class outside to a place where there are a number of puddles. Have them bring with them hand lenses and any other special tools or equipment they think might be helpful to their puddle examinations. This might include clear plastic cups, rulers, thermometers, filter paper, sieves, jars, eye droppers, and so on. All students should bring a pencil, paper, and something to write on such as a clipboard.
3. Students should choose a puddle to observe. Make sure they avoid puddles of stagnant water that might possibly be unhealthy to touch. Obviously, no one should taste the water in any type of puddle. Encourage the students to take detailed notes about their observations on site. When they return to the classroom, they can write up their final "puddle reports."

Assessment Criteria

It is important to let the students know what they will be evaluated on in this assessment. Tell them that you are interested in finding out

✔ **how they go about examining a puddle**
✔ **what different types of observations they make**
✔ **how detailed their observations are**

Prompts for Getting Started

As students make lists of their observations, you might want to ask individuals questions such as these:

- **How is your puddle different from other puddles? What makes it unique?**
- **What could you do to increase the number of your observations?**
- **Can you make your observations more specific and precise?**

Assessing the Work

In this assessment, we are interested in finding out how keen the students' powers of observation are. Do they describe the shape, size, color, smell, clarity, temperature, or location of the puddle? Do they observe with their senses only, or do they use tools to help them increase the accuracy and objectivity of their observations? Do they do any special tests such as seeing what happens when a rock is thrown in the puddle, or taking a sample of puddle water and watching it settle? Do they observe changes or special properties of a puddle such as its reflectiveness or ripples? Some students will be able to think of numerous ways to examine a puddle, while others will struggle to make note of the most obvious characteristics.

Questions to ask yourself while scoring a response:

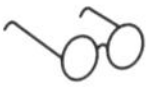

- **How closely does the student examine the puddle? What tools or techniques are used?**
- **What different types of observations does the student make?**
- **Are the observations described in detail?**

Scoring Rubric

Low Response
The puddle observations are limited in nature. Special tools or techniques may not have been used. A few observations are listed, although they may be the most obvious ones. The observations may not be described clearly, accurately, or with much detail.

Medium Response
The puddle has been examined closely, and special tools or techniques may have been used. Several different types of observations are listed. The observations are described fairly clearly and with some detail.

High Response
The puddle has been examined thoughtfully. A rich variety of different types of observations are listed. Special tools and techniques may have been used to gather more information about the puddle. The precise language used in the report makes it easy to visualize the puddle and its contents.

the puddle is 13°C 2 inches deep
4 ft across 3 ft wide. Oil is floting
on the top along with some ded
leaves, tire bits from the playground
have settled on the bottem. Starring
up at me from the puddle is a
distorted figure.
it smells musty and sour
its very quiet it fells wet
Some watter from the puddle colected
in a beker is clear. When a pebble is
droped in it ripels for 5 seckonds,
a pencle stuck in will come
out with this brown dusty-stuff
that clings to it.

top view

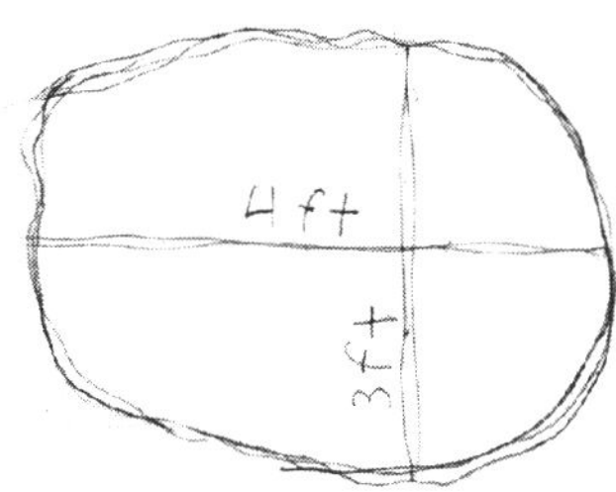

side view

High Response

This student observed the puddle carefully and then organized his data into logical groupings. After giving measurements—length, width, depth, and temperature—the student continues with a description of the puddle. He tells what is in it, top and bottom, and how it looks, smells, and feels. Then he explores the puddle in several ways to gather more information.

High Response

This response includes the circumference of the puddle and a detailed description of its appearance and its contents. The student noted and was interested by the difference between the water at the bottom of the puddle and the water at the top, as well as what happens when the water is disturbed.

Puddle Project

My partener and I examined a puddle. This puddle was 27 cm in circumference. The puddle was very muddy and thick because of the mud. It looked very much like chocolate milk. The puddle water would splash and get all over the container, when it did this it looked very gooey. Many pieces of mud & tanbark were in the puddle, it was very chunky, and seemed as if it was a spider's home because they were a few spiders in there. The puddle water was very thick at the bottom, but extremely thin at the top, it looked as if it was clear. Many pieces of dirt were in this water. After a while the water started to form some bubbles. Also when blown the water would rise like a wave. It was horribly smelly, and had some sort of seeds in it. The puddle water looked like a dark rainy cloud that was so heavy it would explode.

Medium Response

This student's drawing of the puddle shows things she observed that her written description doesn't mention. Her written report could have been more effective if she had included these details. Rather than measuring closely, she estimates the dimensions of the puddle.

Puddle Project

My puddle is kind of in the shape of a rectangle because it is little on both ends, and big in the middle. It has little peices of bark in it because it is right next to the bark area. When it is blowed the water of the puddle swishes back and forth. My estimate of the width is about 20 cm. Tall wise about 5 cm

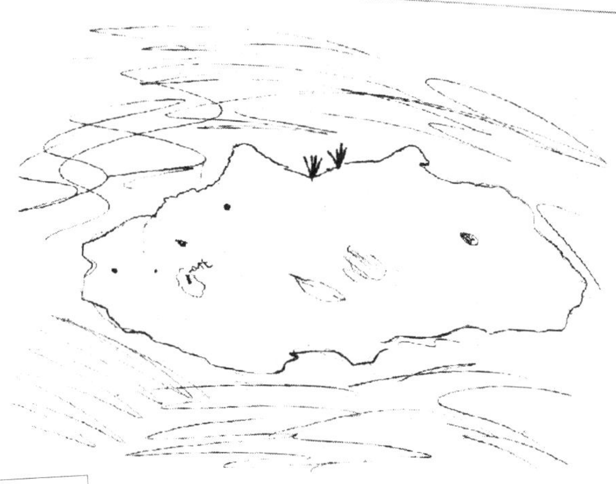

The Puddle Project

1 The mud

a In the puddle was an insect that was white and when it moved, it left a trail in the mud.

b In the mud was algea. Algea grew all over the place. When I tried to scrape it off with a twig, it fell over on it's self.

2 The water

a The water was cold to the touch, and slimy. I rubbed my fingers together and it got oozy!

b The water was full of mud that turned the color of the water brown. Insects swam furiously in every direction, they even swam down!

The Insect

Medium Response

This student organized his response into the two main components of the puddle as he saw it: the mud and the water. He describes the details that interested him most, the living things, and he includes a detailed picture of a creature he saw in the mud.

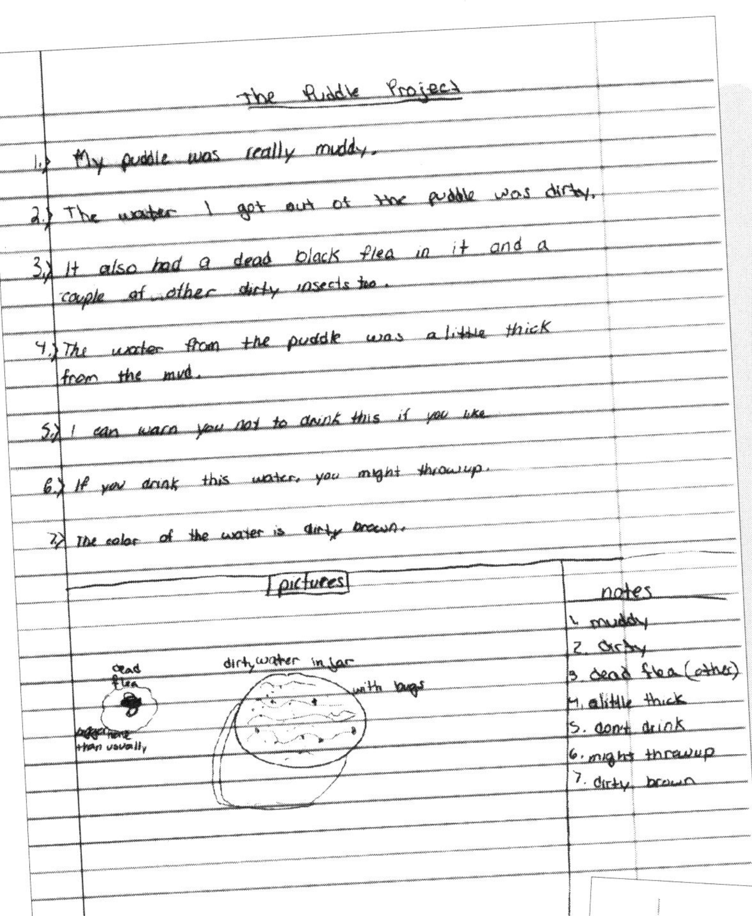

The Puddle Project

1.) My puddle was really muddy.

2.) The water I got out of the puddle was dirty.

3.) It also had a dead black flea in it and a couple of other dirty insects too.

4.) The water from the puddle was a little thick from the mud.

5.) I can warn you not to drink this if you like.

6.) If you drink this water, you might throwup.

7.) The color of the water is dirty brown.

pictures

notes
1. muddy
2. dirty
3. dead flea (other)
4. alittle thick
5. dont drink
6. might threwup
7. dirty brown

Low Response

The seven items listed here are somewhat repetitive because the student has had a hard time coming up with a variety of observations. Two of the items she lists are not observations, but warnings not to drink the water.

The puddle project

The puddle was very dirty. If you are a small creature you would think that the blob of dirt is a mountain that is covered with water. It had black stuff in it and I think that just might be dirt. All kind of stuff is in it. Green mooshy stuff is on it, and plants were on the bottom of it. There are bugs in it and red stuff that is floating above the water. And there is rocks in it too. That was an interesting puddle I experimented.

Low Response

There are few specific descriptive words in this report (*stuff* is used four times), perhaps because the student did not keep field notes as she observed the puddle. She has seen a number of things, but she does not convey that fact effectively.

Extending the Learning

1. Bring the class together to discuss how they went about making their observations and what tools they used.
2. Then have each student pair up with another student who examined a different puddle to read each other's reports. **What kinds of observations did you and your partner make? What are some things that your partner listed that you might have listed for your puddle? What observations did you make that your partner did not?**
3. Ask the pairs to compare and contrast their puddles and the techniques they used to observe them.

~~ Talking It Over ~~

Did you use any special tools or techniques in examining your puddle?

~ I used a ruler. I could have used a tape measure to measure around the puddle, but I couldn't find one.

~ I measured the temperature with a thermometer.

~ I just mostly looked. It seemed like I could find out a lot if I just concentrated. The hand lens helped a lot, too.

~ I looked for a while, but then I tried some things like dropping stuff in the puddle and blowing on the water to see what happened. If I had a fan, I could tell even more about how the water moves.

~ A lot of people used plastic cups to take the water out and look at it. It was weird how it looked really clear in the cup, when it looked so dirty on the ground.

~ That depends on where you scooped the water. If you touched the bottom of the puddle, it was pretty muddy.

~ Right, but if you leave the water in the cup, the mud falls down and the water on the top is clear. That's why it looks clear if you just take it from the top of the puddle.

~ It looks clear, but it's still pretty disgusting. It's not like the sink water.

~ How can you tell?

Good question. What tools and techniques could you use to compare the puddle water to the water in the sink?

Follow-Up Activity

1. Have the students reread their reports and think about all of the ways in which the information in the report would change over time. Ask the students to make some predictions. **How long do you think it will take for your puddle to evaporate completely?**
2. Revisit the puddles each day until they have evaporated completely. At the time of each visit, have the students record the changes they observe in their puddle's size and shape as well as other characteristics such as the clarity of the water. **Record all of the ways in which your puddle has changed.** If it rains during the observation period, the students might want to measure the amount of rain that falls and see how that amount relates to the size of the puddle.

Observe and Classify

In this investigation, students are asked to devise a classification system for everything they see around them in an outdoor setting. Developing a system that is comprehensive, logical, and understandable is an extremely challenging task. The most successful systems students come up with are likely to feature branching diagrams of some sort, since this format allows classification from the general to the specific, and highlights the complex relationships among diagram elements. Many students, though, will select simpler ways of thinking about and classifying their list items.

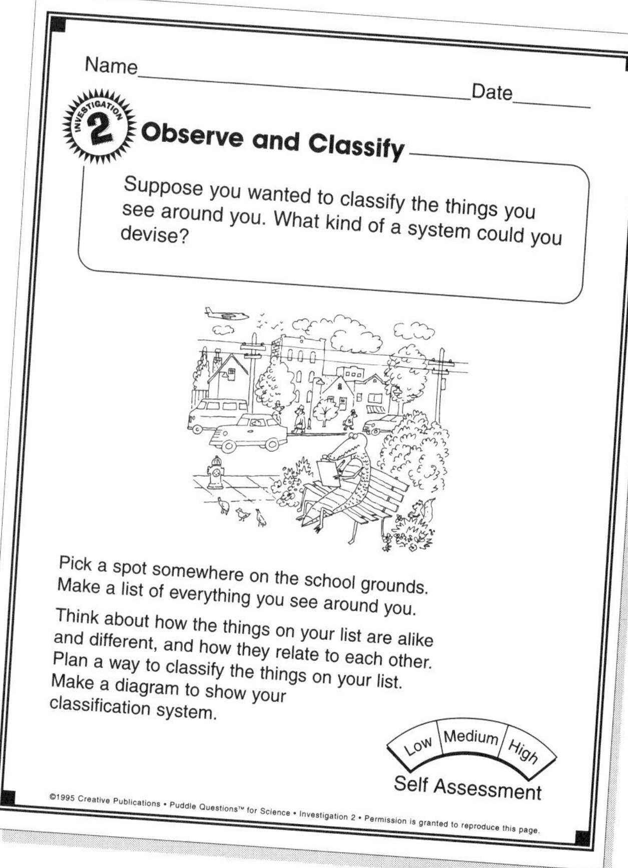

Name____________________ Date________

Observe and Classify

Suppose you wanted to classify the things you see around you. What kind of a system could you devise?

Pick a spot somewhere on the school grounds. Make a list of everything you see around you.

Think about how the things on your list are alike and different, and how they relate to each other. Plan a way to classify the things on your list. Make a diagram to show your classification system.

Low Medium High
Self Assessment

©1995 Creative Publications • Puddle Questions™ for Science • Investigation 2 • Permission is granted to reproduce this page.

Blackline Master in English, page 79
and in Spanish, page 80

Science Processes

- Observing characteristics
- Comparing likenesses and differences
- Devising classification systems

Tools and Equipment

- ◆ blank paper
- ◆ lined writing paper
- ◆ pencils

Grouping Arrangement

Individuals

Time Frame

About an hour

Presenting the Investigation

1. Pass out copies of the investigation and explain to the students that their challenge will be to create a classification system for the things they see outside.
2. Take the class outside, and have each student select an "observation post." **Look at all the things you see around you. How are they similar or different? Which things go together in some way?** Ask the students to carefully observe their surroundings, and to begin to make a list of the things they see.
3. As students work on their lists, they should be thinking about how they might organize or classify the items. The point at which different students shift from list making to developing their classification schemes will vary, depending on how confident they feel about the classification scheme they are imagining. Encourage the students to develop systems that are comprehensive. Each of the items on their list should fit somewhere in their classification scheme.

Assessment Criteria

It is important to let students know what they will be evaluated on in this assessment. Tell them that you are interested in finding out

✔ **how detailed their observations are**
✔ **how comprehensive, complex, and workable their system is**
✔ **whether items are grouped logically**
✔ **how they use charts or diagrams to make their classification system clear to others**

Prompts for Getting Started

Questions like these can help students to get started on the investigation or to continue working when they are stuck:

- **What kinds of things are on your list so far?**
- **How could you organize your list? Which things go together? In what way?**
- **How can you show your system in a way that's easy for others to understand?**

Assessing the Work

This is an assessment of students' abilities to see the relationships among a wide-ranging set of items, and to devise classification systems to convey those relationships. Some students will organize the items on their list into broad, unrelated categories, while others will develop many levels of interrelated categories for their classification schemes.

Questions to ask yourself while scoring a response:

- **How detailed has the student's observation of his surroundings been?**
- **How comprehensive and complex is the classification system?**
- **Does the system show the relationships between the items on the list?**
- **Is the system presented clearly?**

Scoring Rubric

Low Response
A simple organizational scheme is developed, which may be based on a limited list of items. Organization may be driven by a single, general attribute (color, for instance), or the items may be organized according to unrelated categories, so that the system does not address the relationships among the listed items.

Medium Response
An attempt has been made to develop a classification system that conveys the relationships among the items on the list. The system is presented clearly, but may lack detail or comprehensiveness.

High Response
A comprehensive and logical classification scheme is developed to accommodate an extensive list of diverse items. The system effectively conveys the complex relationships among the items through an intricate branching diagram that progresses from broad to specific categories.

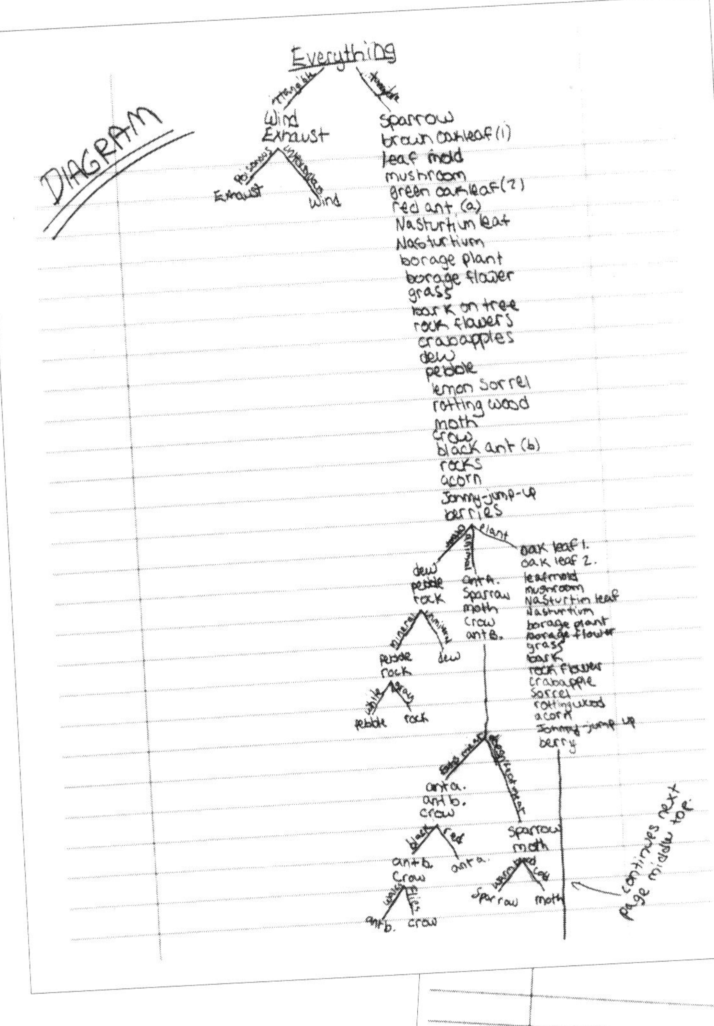

High Response

This extremely comprehensive and complex branching diagram begins with the most general category this student can imagine: "Everything." It then divides each category into more and more specific categories, carefully including all the items from the student's original list that fit each subcategory.

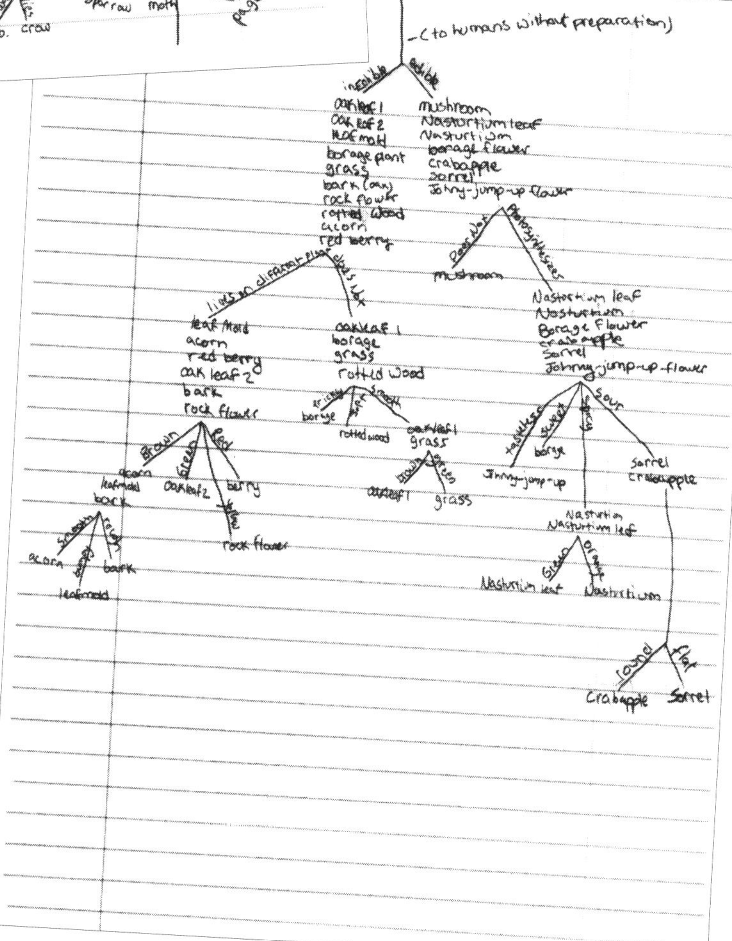

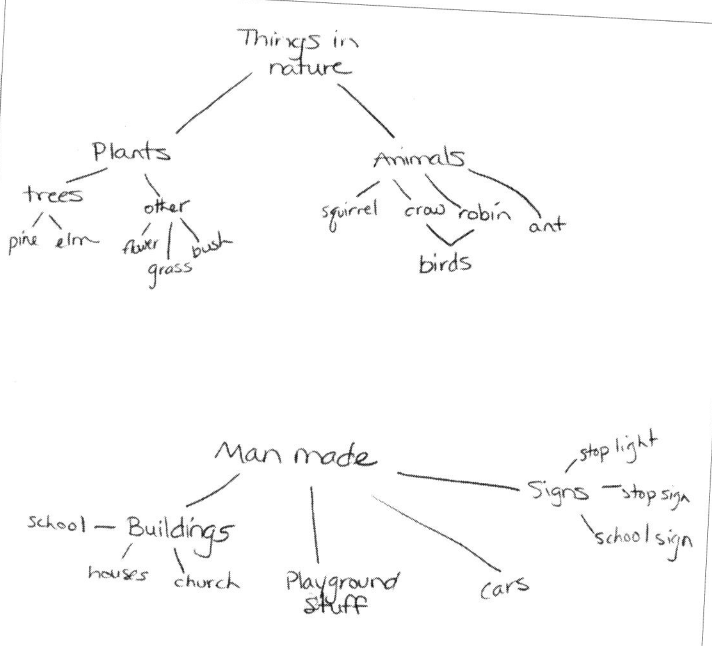

Medium Response

The approach taken by this student is logical and hierarchical. She wasn't able to weave all the items on her list into this scheme, however, and the categories she uses are not always as descriptive as they could be.

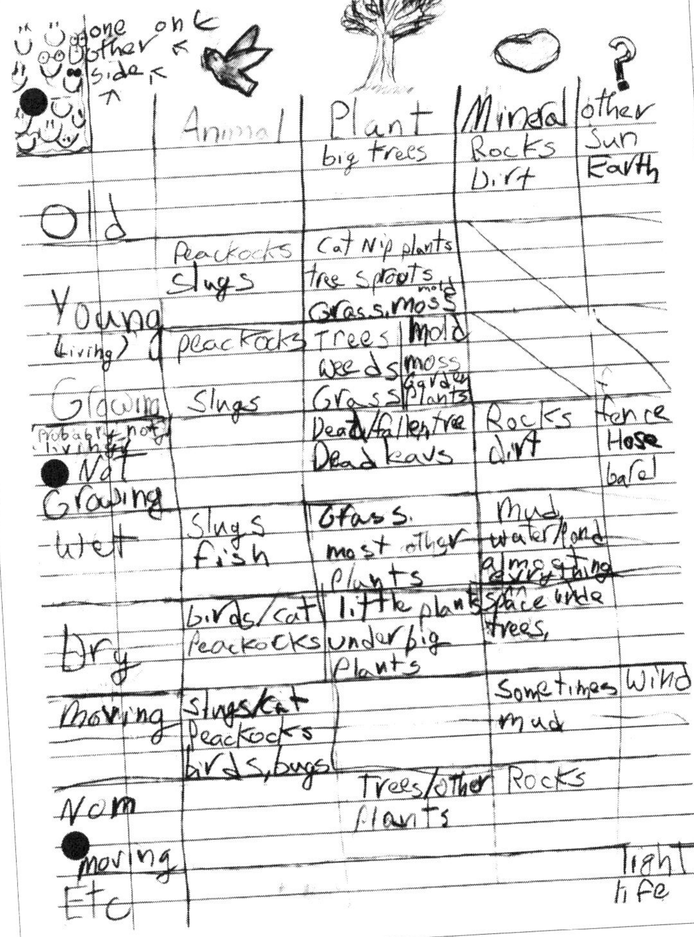

Medium Response

Working from a limited observation list, this student comes up with an interesting classification system. She uses the categories "animal," "plant," "mineral," and "other" as the main organizers for her system, and then chooses several pairs of opposite attributes as the categories along the vertical axis of her chart.

Clear	RED	WHITE	GREEN	BLUE	BLACK	OTHER
window	My shirt	house	grass	sky	Mud	tree trunk
air	sign	car	Leaf's	car	road	paper bag
heat	car	clouds	tree top		My Folder	Pencil
cold					My Shirt	Steps
glasses						

Low Response

This student groups the items on his list according to color—an unsophisticated classification scheme based on a single property.

1. Trees
A. Birch
B. Cherry
C. maple
D. Spruce *

2. Garages
A. Yellow
B. White *
C. Brown
D. Grey
E. Brick

3. Houses
A. Brown
B. White
C. Yellow
D. Grey
E. Peach
F. blue
G. Half brick

4. Animals
A. Squirls
B. Birds *
C. Dog
D. Women *

5. Flowers
A. Roses
B. marigold
C. Impatients
D. unknown kinds *

6. Thing on trees
A. Leaves
B. branchs
C. pine needles
D. bark

7. Things on the ground
A. grass
B. dirt
C. Cement
d. floor mat
E. Plants
F. Gardens

8. Person made things
A. big wheel
B. T.V. antenas
C. Chairs
D. Cars
E. Electrical box
F. Bird bath *
G. Swing set
H. Telophone poll
I. Fences

Low Response

For the most part, the categories chosen by this student lack parallelism, and she hasn't attempted to indicate relationships among the categories.

Extending the Learning

1. Get the class together to talk about the processes they went through while developing their classification systems. Students who are interested may explain their systems to the class. Questions such as the following can help guide the discussion: **Once you'd made your list, how did you decide on a way to classify the items? What steps did you go through to devise a workable system? Did the first system you tried work?**
2. Make overhead transparencies of selected student classification schemes and display them on the overhead projector. It will be interesting for students to see the variety of diagrams their classmates used to organize their systems. Even diagrams of the same type can be quite different, depending on the categories and subcategories chosen.
3. Have the students analyze each scheme in terms of how comprehensive it is, whether or not it highlights relationships among the listed items, and how clearly the system is communicated. After discussing the strengths and weaknesses of the systems, students may be able to propose ideas for making the systems more effective.

~~ Talking It Over ~~

What kinds of things do you need to think about when designing a classification system?

~ You look at all the things on your list and see what they have in common. You probably find out there would be lots of different ways of organizing the stuff, but I just tried to pick the best way.

~ At first I looked at my list and tried to see which things went together, and what kinds of categories there were.

~ I started with the categories "animals," "plants," and "other." But since plants and animals are both living things, I decided to use "living" and "nonliving" instead. That made more sense.

~ I made three different classification systems. One went by "man-made" or "natural," one went by "living" or "nonliving," and one went by "solid," "liquid," or "gas."

~ I used "things from nature" and "things made by humans" to start with. Then I saw that I could break those groups down, too.

Follow-Up Activity

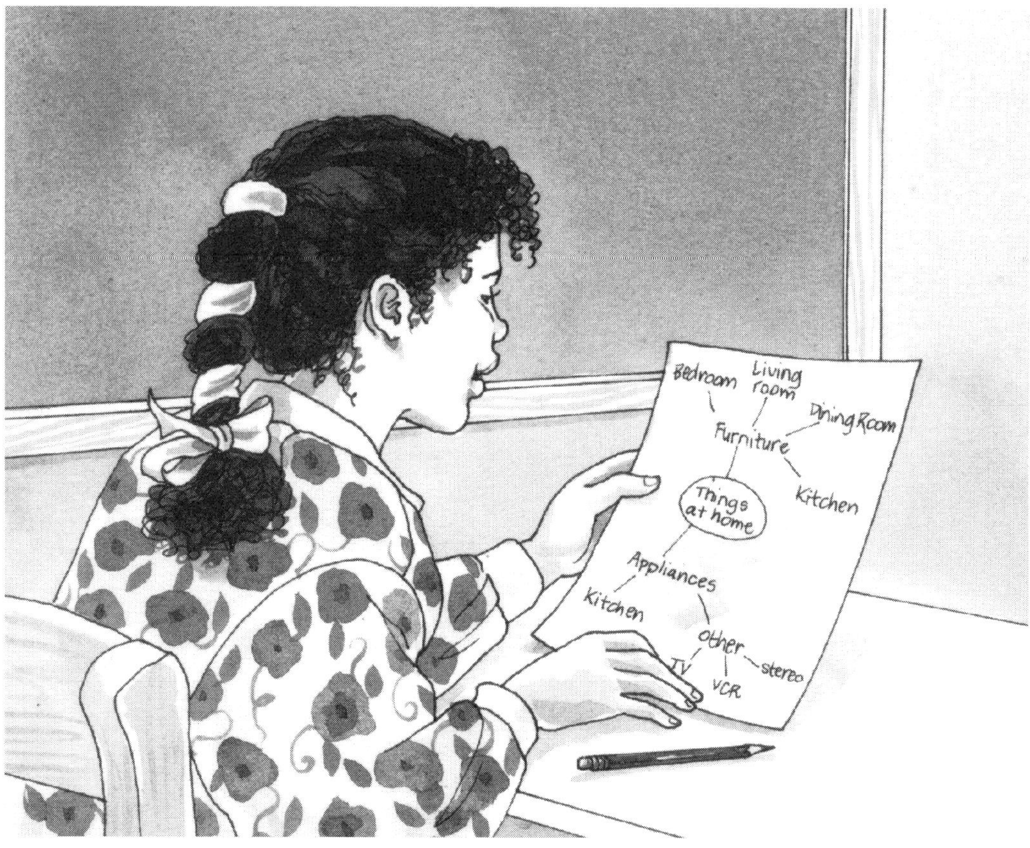

1. Invite the students to devise a system for classifying everything in their homes. Students are likely to have developed their thinking a bit during the class discussion period, and they may have new thoughts about how to develop an effective classification system, or how to refine the type of system they initially designed. The focus here should be on devising categories and branching subcategories that could include all the items in a home, rather than on specific items (spoons, vases, and so on). Since this may be a challenge to some students, be prepared to help them through the initial struggle.
2. Students can take their completed systems home with them to see how successful they are. Remind the students that there should be a place in the classification scheme for every kind of item found at home. Some students may revise their systems based on their observations.
3. Make a display of all the students' final "at home" classification schemes. It will be interesting to discuss together the many different systems and how they work.

Landscaping Plans

In this investigation, students are asked to conduct research to find plants that would beautify their school grounds and be appropriate for the available growing conditions. Besides learning how to use resource books, students must decide what plant characteristics are desirable for their area, then track down suitable plants. If your school lacks a potential garden area, you can modify the investigation by suggesting that your students select plants that could be grown in containers or a nearby vacant lot.

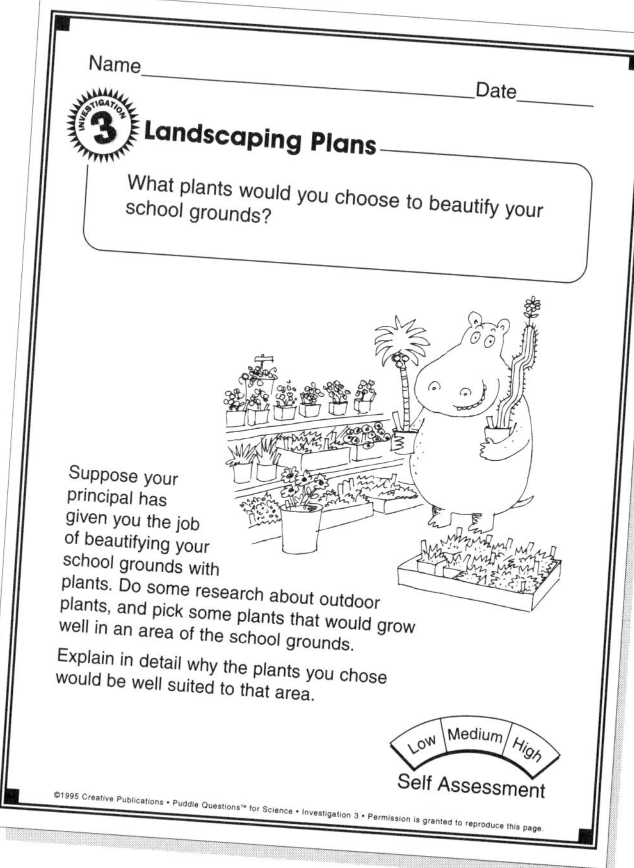

Name______________________________ Date__________

INVESTIGATION 3 **Landscaping Plans**

What plants would you choose to beautify your school grounds?

Suppose your principal has given you the job of beautifying your school grounds with plants. Do some research about outdoor plants, and pick some plants that would grow well in an area of the school grounds.

Explain in detail why the plants you chose would be well suited to that area.

Low | Medium | High

Self Assessment

Blackline Master in English, page 81
and in Spanish, page 82

Science Processes

- Conducting research
- Applying information in real-life contexts

Tools and Equipment

- resource books on plants, gardening, and landscaping
- blank paper
- lined writing paper
- pencils

Grouping Arrangement

Individuals or pairs

Time Frame

$1\frac{1}{2}$ to 2 hours

Presenting the Investigation

1. Pass out copies of the investigation and explain to the students that their task is to do some research about outdoor plants in order to select some that would be well suited to the conditions on your school grounds. Point out the resource books you have gathered. **Use these books to research outdoor plants. Try to identify some plants that you think would grow well in a particular area on our school grounds.**
2. Some students may focus on shrubs or small ornamental trees, while others may decide to select flowers. As they work, students may be thinking about factors such as what the local climate is like, how the sun hits various parts of the school grounds, how much rain your area gets in different seasons, the time of year particular flowers bloom, and so on.
3. Have the students write reports listing the plants they have selected, and explaining why they believe those plants to be well suited to the school grounds.

Assessment Criteria

It is important to let students know what they will be evaluated on in this assessment. Tell them that you are interested in finding out

- ✔ **how thoroughly they research landscaping options and the selected plants**
- ✔ **the reasons they give for selecting particular plants**
- ✔ **how well suited the chosen plants are to the available growing conditions**

Prompts for Getting Started

Questions such as the following may be helpful to students who are having difficulty knowing where to start:

- **What is the climate like in our area? How could you find out whether a particular plant would grow well here?**
- **How are the resource books you plan to use organized? How could you find the information you need in order to decide on appropriate plants for our school grounds?**

Assessing the Work

This is an assessment of students' abilities to conduct research and apply the collected information to a specific problem. As students conduct their research, they'll need to make note of pertinent facts and evaluate the information, making inferences about how (or whether) each particular plant would flourish if planted on the school grounds. Your observations of the effort various students put into the research portion of this project will be helpful as you assess their work on this investigation.

Questions to ask yourself while scoring a response:

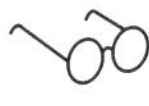

- **How thoroughly have different options been explored before a plant selection was made?**
- **Were resources used effectively to find pertinent information on plants and suggested growing conditions?**
- **Are sound reasons given for selecting particular plants? Are the chosen plants well suited to the available growing conditions?**

Scoring Rubric

Low Response
Some research has been done, but very little of the information gathered has been applied to the plant selection. Plant selection may have been based on aesthetics or personal preference rather than on an understanding of appropriate growing conditions.

Medium Response
Some research has been conducted, and an effort has been made to apply some of the information to the problem at hand. The rationale for selecting particular plants may lack detail.

High Response
Focused and thorough research has been conducted, and the information gathered has been carefully applied to the plant selection process. Detailed reasons for selecting particular plants are included.

What plants would you use to beautify your school?

Trees

I think that we should have Holy Leaf Cherry trees. They're tall and have cherries. I choose this tree because it is extremely drought-tolerant. It can survive in all zones except high elevations and deserts. It can conserve water.

Another tree is the Portugal Laurel. I choose this one because it is colorful. It is not very tall. It will be good in our garden because sun can go through it to shine on the flowers.

Flowers

I chose the California Poppy because it is colorful and grows just about everywhere. It doesn't need much water and it is easy to maintain. It grows well in California.

Ground Covers

I chose the Scaevola 'Mauve Cluster' because they are drough-tolerant and are determined by the U.S Agricultural Department to grow

High Response

This student and his partner did extensive research in order to make their final selections. They paid careful attention to the climate in their area, and approved only plants that were appropriate to their "zone." A map of the garden they envision shows how they would arrange their chosen plants.

area. They sunlight and moderate watering will take up about 3 feet of space.

also chose Genistu flowers because ke little water and don't need good soil. It is also guranteed by the U.S. Agricultural Department to grow well in our area. It needs sunlight and takes up about 2 feet of space.

Shrubs

Ceanothus Thysiflorus - Sky lark blue blossom, It's 4-6 feet tall. There are clusters of dark blue flowers covering the plant throughout spring. Characteristics are flowers and evergreen. Water monthly and well drain soil

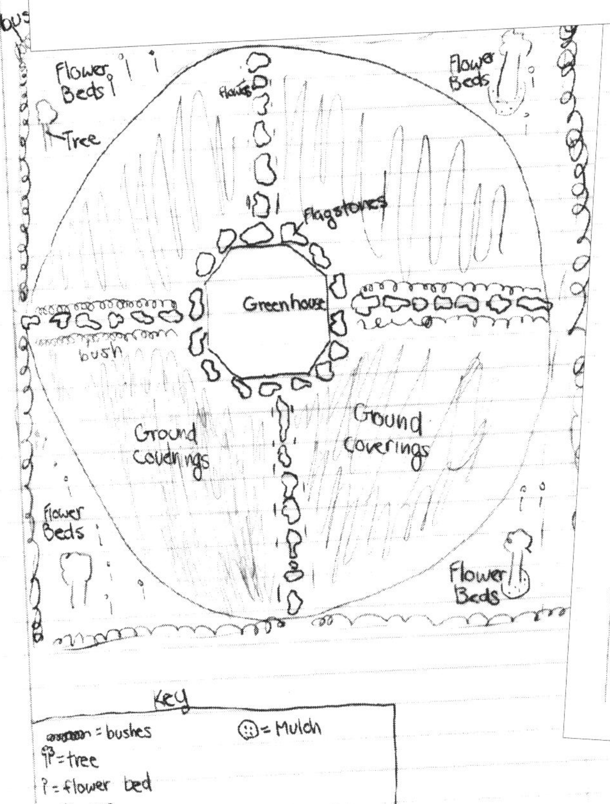

What plants would you choose to beautify your school grounds?

My portener and I decided that we wanted to plant a california poppy as one of our plants becaus it can grow in all zones. It is also very pretty and we could make the colors match with all of the other plants because it can be yellow, orange, red, pink, white, and multi-colors. It is best to plant it in fall so if we planted it right away then it would probably do very well. It blooms for a medium amount of time, which is okay but not perfect. It doesn't take much water because it is a native California plant and california has had a drought for a long time so the poppy has gotten used to it. It is a very pretty flower and it would look nice in our school's garden.

Our next flower is a Caryoptris. It is Autumn flowering shrub. We picked this because it needs little water and it is a good contrast with the poppy. The flower grows well in a 5-9 zone and we live in a 9 zone. This flower is a beautiful shade of blue and can't stand cold winters but, in Palo Alto we don't get very cold winters.

High Response

After a good deal of research, this student and her partner selected several plants. Besides being interested in choosing colors that would look nice together, they paid careful attention to climatic considerations. The four-page report (only one of which is shown here) includes a summary, a bibliography, and a map showing where the three plants selected would be placed.

Investigation 3: Landscaping

What plants would you choose to beautify your school grounds?

Flowers

1. Primula Polyantha is an all year round flower. It can be found in all differerent colors- red, orange, yellow, green, blue, purple, and white. Can survive anywhere.
2. Gazanias require only a little water and sunshine. They are red, orange, yellow, pink, and white. Drought tolerant.
3. Dietas Vegeta produces white 3 inch flowers with orange and brown markings. Drought tolerant

Write up

I picked these flowers because they all could survive in this climate, and they all don't need very much water. Primula Polyantha might need more than the Gazanias and the Dietas Vegeta, but it won't be to much more.

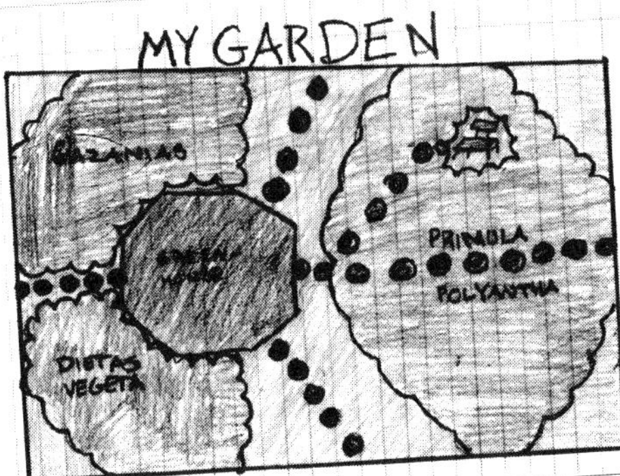

Medium Response

This student used one book on drought-resistant plants and quickly selected several flowers from it. The amount of water the plants need was the only factor taken into account.

Investagation Question

Nigella

The Nigella is one-and a half inch, it opens its blossems on plants 1 foot tall. The colors are blue, white, rose, pink and purple. And is a fennel flower. We choose this flower because it was very pretty. The Nigella dosen't need much to stay alive. We decided to place the Nigella 2 feet in front of the wall. We choose this place because it needs a lot of sun. The Nigella needs a full amount of sun. It also is tolerent to all types of soil. To plant the Nigella you need to sow the seeds in the soil. You need to plant it in the spring but in mild places you can plant it in the fall.

Medium Response

Nigella is chosen by this student primarily for aesthetic reasons. Several details such as this plant's tolerance of various soils and its need for full sun are also taken into consideration. However, the placement of the Nigella near the wall is unlikely to give it as much sun as the student says it needs.

Investagation 3: Landscaping
What plants would you choose to school grounds

Name: Baileya multiradiata

Hieght: 1'

Bloom: Possible year

Expoposure: Full sun/very light shade

Soil: Any with good drainage.

I like this plant because it can bloom all year round.

I think this type of flower can survive here because it needs light, and, and it needs little water

Low Response

Minimal research was done by this student. Most of the information in the report is quoted directly from a research book. This particular desert plant, which thrives in arid regions, is not well suited to the climate in this student's area.

Extending the Learning

1. Gather the class together to discuss their work on the investigation. Have volunteers tell about one or two plants they selected, and explain how they determined that those plants would grow well on the school grounds.
2. Ask the students to describe their research processes. **How did you use the resource books to decide which plants to choose? How were the books you used organized? What types of information were helpful to you in making your selections?**

~~ Talking It Over ~~

What was your research process like? How did you go about making your plant selections?

~ We were using the Sunset *Western Garden Book*. At first we were just reading through the A–Z list of plants. Then we noticed this thing about zones. We had to look through the introduction to find out what that meant.

~ We did that, too. In the front there are a bunch of maps and it's divided into zones. You find out which zone you live in, then any plants that have that zone number can grow in your area.

~ We wanted to find plants that didn't need much water because of the drought. So we looked through the books and found something about low-water-use plants.

~ We wanted to find flowers that would bloom during the school year so we'd be around when they were colorful. We read the descriptions of different flowers, and found some that bloom in the fall, and others for the spring. That way, we're covered all year.

~ We thought we had ours all decided on, but then we read that Nigellas need full sun. The place we were thinking of doing our garden has lots of shady spots. So we had to start looking for things that could grow in partial shade.

Follow-Up Activity

1. Have the students take their research one step farther. **Imagine you were actually going to plant your plants at school. What would you need to do to guarantee that they would flourish?**
2. Have the students research suggestions for the care of their chosen plants and then outline a detailed plan for taking care of them. Students might want to consider including information about exactly where the plants should be planted, how much space they would need, how much water they take and how often, the amount of sun they are best suited to, and any additional maintenance (pruning, pinching back, etc.) they might require.
3. It might also be interesting to invite a landscape architect to visit your class to talk about how a professional would go about deciding what plants to use for a particular site. Your students could then share with the landscaper the plant choices they made for the school grounds, and get his or her opinion about their selections.

Paper Bridges

In this investigation, students apply their knowledge of physical science to the problem of building the strongest bridge they can with just one piece of paper. Strength here is defined by how many pennies the bridge can support. What at first may seem to students an impossible task quickly turns into the challenge of finding the shape and size that maximizes the use of the paper. You may find you are surprised by how strong a single sheet of paper can be!

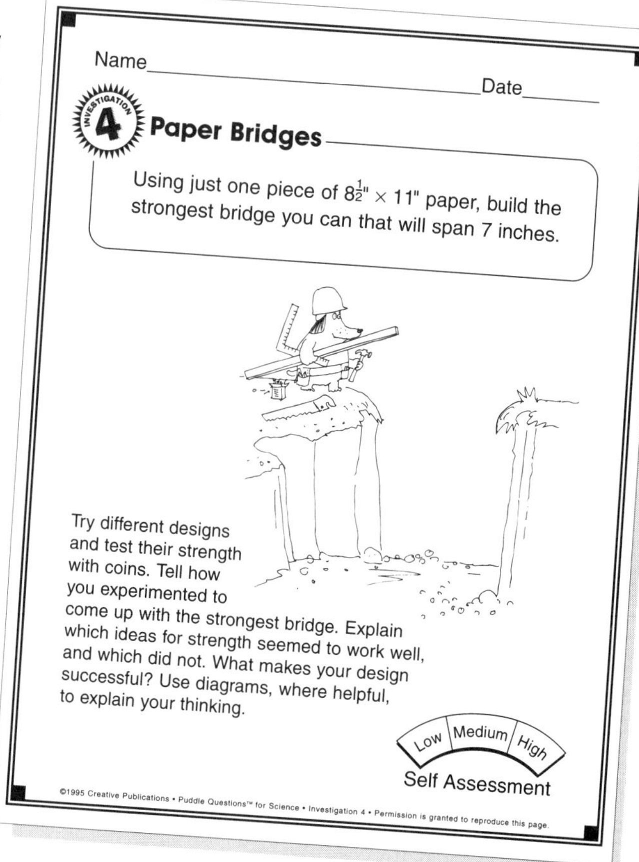
Name_______________ Date_______

4 Paper Bridges

Using just one piece of $8\frac{1}{2}$" × 11" paper, build the strongest bridge you can that will span 7 inches.

Try different designs and test their strength with coins. Tell how you experimented to come up with the strongest bridge. Explain which ideas for strength seemed to work well, and which did not. What makes your design successful? Use diagrams, where helpful, to explain your thinking.

Low Medium High
Self Assessment

Blackline Master in English, page 83
and in Spanish, page 84

Science Processes

- Testing hypotheses
- Optimizing outcomes

Tools and Equipment

- $8\frac{1}{2}$" × 11" scrap paper
- a large supply of pennies or other weights
- scissors
- tape
- rulers
- blank paper
- lined writing paper
- pencils

Grouping Arrangement

Pairs or small groups

Time Frame

2–3 hours

Presenting the Investigation

1. Have students arrange their desks so that there is a 7-inch gap between pairs of desks. Show the students a piece of $8\frac{1}{2}$" × 11" paper from your recycling bin and pose the following question: **Suppose you wanted to build a bridge to span the distance between your desks. How could you build the strongest bridge possible out of just one piece of paper?**
2. Encourage students to experiment with paper to find ways to make strong bridges, and then test each bridge by seeing how many coins it will support. Cutting, folding, and taping the paper are fine, but tell the students that the ends of their bridges must rest on the desks without being taped down. Tape should be used only to maintain a desired shape, not to strengthen the bridge.
3. Talk a little about how the students will use the coins to test their bridges for strength. An important rule is that the coins must be placed on the span itself, not on the part of the bridge that overlaps the desks. You may decide that the coins can be placed anywhere on the span, or you may prefer a rule that the pennies can only be stacked in one pile in the center of the bridge. Stacking the pennies in the center will take many fewer pennies, an advantage if your class is short on coins.
4. Have plenty of scrap paper handy for this exploration. Students should feel free to experiment with a number of ideas without feeling that they are being wasteful of paper. Observe how students explore different approaches and test for strength.
5. Have the students write about the different ideas they tried, and how many coins each bridge held. Encourage them to write about what does or doesn't work to create a strong bridge.

Assessment Criteria

It is important to let the students know what they will be evaluated on in this assessment. Tell them that you are interested in finding out

- ✔ **the ways in which they experiment with materials and designs**
- ✔ **how strong their strongest bridge is**
- ✔ **whether they can make any generalizations about strong bridge designs from what they learn in their explorations**

Prompts for Getting Started

Questions such as these can help students continue working when they get stuck:

- **What do you think is causing your bridge to collapse?**
- **Can you think of a way to make your bridge even stronger?**
- **What is a completely different way to make your bridge?**

Assessing the Work

This is an assessment of students' abilities to experiment with a problem in order to optimize outcomes. Along the way, they'll need to be analyzing possibilities and testing ideas about what factors might increase the strength of the bridge. The bridges students create, the reports they write, and the observations you make as they work are all important in evaluating an individual student's performance on this assessment task.

Questions to ask yourself while scoring a response:

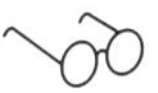

- **Does the student try various approaches to creating a strong bridge?**
- **How many coins does the student's bridge hold?**
- **Does the student draw any conclusions from the explorations?**

Scoring Rubric

Low Response
The student may have given up easily after trying only one approach. The student's strongest bridge holds relatively few pennies, or its strength may rely on unacceptable methods such as taping the bridge to the desks. Little is reported about what the student has learned from the investigation.

Medium Response
More than one design idea has been tried, or the student has tried various ways to improve on one design idea. The student's strongest bridge holds a moderate number of pennies. Conclusions drawn may be fairly obvious.

High Response
Good design ideas have been used to create several different bridges, the strongest of which holds a relatively large number of coins. Comparisons are made among the bridge designs, and conclusions drawn are reasonable.

Science Experiment

Today Miss K—'s class conducted an experiment. We tried to build a bridge out of paper that would hold as many pennies as possible. There were certain restrictions though. We could only use one piece of paper and tape. The bridge had to be seven inches in length.

At first I thought this experiment was going to be easy. I had done this at a camp over the summer. The key was to make it wide and thin. Though the experiment was who could get the most washers in tinfoil without it sinking. As it turned out ,it was the complete opposite. The key to making this experiment work was to double layer it and make think, high walls.

The first bridge I built showed me my theory was wrong. I had made a single layered piece of paper with barely any walls. (shown in fig. 1)

As I tried it out, it didn't turn out quite as I expected. It only held 47 pennies.

The second bridge I did with D—. We double layered the bottom and walls. (shown in fig. 2)

☆ fig 2 (bird's eye view)

This turned out a lot better than I expected. It held 162 pennies and probably could have held more, but someone accidently moved the table and caused it to move.

The third bridge I did with my sister at hove. I took my new theory into mind and created a bridge which was double layered and had pretty tall walls. This time I added a crease in the middle and tripled layered the ends of the wall. (shown in fig. 3)

☆ fig3

This didn't work as well as bridge #2. It held 143 pennies. I think it didn't work as well because the sides weren't tall enough.

I've learned many things from this experiment. The most important thing I learned was that things aren't always what they seem, for example scientific theories might apply to one object and not to another. This information might be useful when I grow up because it teaches me not to jump to conclusions and take people's word, but to test it out and make sure. I also learned that paper is not the best material for building a bridge, even for pennies.

☆ shaded part refers to walls

High Response

A similar experiment done with different materials in the past led this student to one conclusion that, to her credit, she was able to revise based on new evidence. Her generalization that double layering and high walls make for a good strong bridge is substantiated in her results from testing three different bridge ideas. Her experience with this investigation taught her an important lesson—not to jump to conclusions in scientific research.

High Response

This student was the first in her class to create a bridge idea that worked at all. Although modest compared to her second attempt, this first bridge idea worked because of the added length she was able to achieve by rolling the paper up on the diagonal. Her second design idea, a funnel effect, provided a secure pocket for holding the penny weights. Even stuffed full of pennies, this bridge held.

I had a problem. I had to build a bridge that could hold as many pennies as possible using one piece of 8 by 11 inch paper with only tape to hold things together.

I came up with two ideas. One used no tape which held 70 pennies and the other used little tape but held 300 pennies. The difference was that one was stacking and the other was stuffing. To make the first one you just roll the paper at a diagonal to make it longer and stronger than just one piece of paper sitting over a edge. The second one I rolled the paper up to be like a funnel. After stuffing it full of pennies, it still wouldn't collapse, so I started stacking more pennies on top. After a little while they all fell off the top of the paper.

I learned that the paper can be very thin but can hold a lot of weight if folded properly. The thing that we had to think about most was how to make the bridge not collapse under all that weight without a lot of support.

#1 #2

Today I did an experiment making bridges. The only things we could use, were paper and some tape(only to hold the paper together). It was kind of hard to find the best way to make a paper bridge, but after experimenting with different models, I kind of knew what I was doing.

I got a piece of paper to make my first bridge. I folded the paper in half. Then, I folded about one inch from both sides inward to make rails. Then I started placing coins on the bridge. After nine pennies, the bridge had fallen down. Already I had learned something. I learned that if the bridge is thin and weak, it will not hold a lot of weight.

Next I made a new bridge. For this bridge I took the paper and folded it up until it was only about two centimeters wide. Then, again I folded the sides inward, this time only about half of a centimeter. My new bridge was finished. Since my bridge was only wide enough to hold the width of one penny, I stacked the pennies in piles of five. One, two, three. I ended up with seventeen piles. That's a total of 85 pennies! I was very surprised.

My conclusion is this. You have to have a strong bridge to hold a lot of weight.

Medium Response

It was a genuine surprise to this student that she could create a bridge that held so many pennies (85). Like her first bridge, her second one has railings, but it is much narrower—exactly one penny wide.

Science
The Bridge

My experimented about my bridge is that first I take a white paper and fold it three times. Then I taped around the paper about 5 minutes and put it between two dest about 7 inches. I piles the pennies till it to 102 and everything start to falling down.

The best ideas that seemed to work is to fold the paper in some kind of shape and use tapes. The ideas that seemed not working well it not to let anything hold the paper and never made the paper as strong as you can.

My design make it successful is I fold lots of times and tape it a lot and that what makes the paper span strongly.

Low Response

This student tried only one design idea, and its strength is based almost entirely on the huge amount of tape she wound around the paper. The bridge is only $8\frac{1}{2}$ inches long, so even with the tape, the bridge toppled after 102 pennies were added.

I'm reporting on a brige report. The 6th Graders tried to make a brige with a 7 inch support span I did 2 differnt experiments.

My first experiment: I took 4 books and staked them on each other and put a paper in the middle. This diseny clasped at the first penny.

My second experiment: I took 6 world books and stake three then I folded the paper and renforced it with tape and this dising held 11 pennies.

1 2

Low Response

While this student tried two design ideas, both depend on unacceptable techniques for their strength. In the first, the paper is held between books in a stack. The second bridge is reinforced with tape. Neither bridge holds many pennies.

Extending the Learning

1. Display each group's strongest bridge, labeled with the number of coins it can hold, for everyone to admire. **Look at all the bridges. In what ways are the bridges that held the most pennies alike?**
2. Compare the different design ideas students used. Have students explain how they made their bridges. Talk about what they learned as they worked on their structures.

~~ Talking It Over ~~

What design ideas worked? What didn't?

~ If you fold the paper over lots of times, and make it really thick, it works best.

~ Yeah. Skinny and thick work better than thin and wide.

~ Mine was not skinny and thick but it worked really good. I folded the paper from both sides into the middle and taped it. It made a nice pocket where all the pennies could fit.

~ I made mine like a burrito. I ran out of room in it for pennies, but it never collapsed.

~ I made a triangular tunnel. I learned that if I put five pennies in the right end, I had to put five in the left end so it would balance.

~ That's right! When I got a lot of pennies on my bridge I sweated out every penny I added. I did not want to have too many pennies in one spot on the bridge.

What self-assessment score did you give yourself and why?

~ I gave myself a High because I took other knowledge that I had and I applied it. For example, I knew that if a bridge supported itself it would be really strong, so I tried it.

~ I gave myself a High, too, because I made my own design up. It's different than anyone else's and works pretty good, too.

~ I didn't think I should give myself a High because it wasn't that neat.

~ I gave myself a Medium because I was thinking too hard about how a bridge would really look. I know that real bridges can hold lots of weight. So when I made my bridge look so realistic, it just was too heavy for the space between the desks.

Follow-Up Activity

1. Tell students that they will have a chance to construct another strong bridge, but this time they may choose from a variety of materials. Have them work in small groups. Provide books on how bridges are built, or have students visit the library. Let them do some reading, note taking, and discussing in their groups before they begin to build.
2. Make available a variety of materials for construction (straws, pipe cleaners, insulated wire, craft sticks, tagboard, string, glue, scissors, tape, and so on). Whether students use one material or a combination, their goal is still to build the strongest bridge with a seven-inch span.
3. When the bridges are ready, have students test them as in the investigation. Then discuss the attributes of the strongest structures. What do students think gave them their strength—the materials used, the dimensions of the bridge, the construction methods? **Can you make any generalizations about strong bridges from this experience?**

Hanging by a Thread

In this investigation, students are challenged to create a pendulum that swings 60 times per minute. They may change anything about their pendulum that they think will help them reach the target rate. Students are likely to explore factors such as size and weight of the bob; type or length of the string; and distance through which the pendulum travels (changed by releasing the bob at different heights). The principles of pendulums are not intuitively obvious, so this exploration provides a nice context within which students may use their logical thinking skills to analyze and compare results of various trials, and then determine what the next step should be.

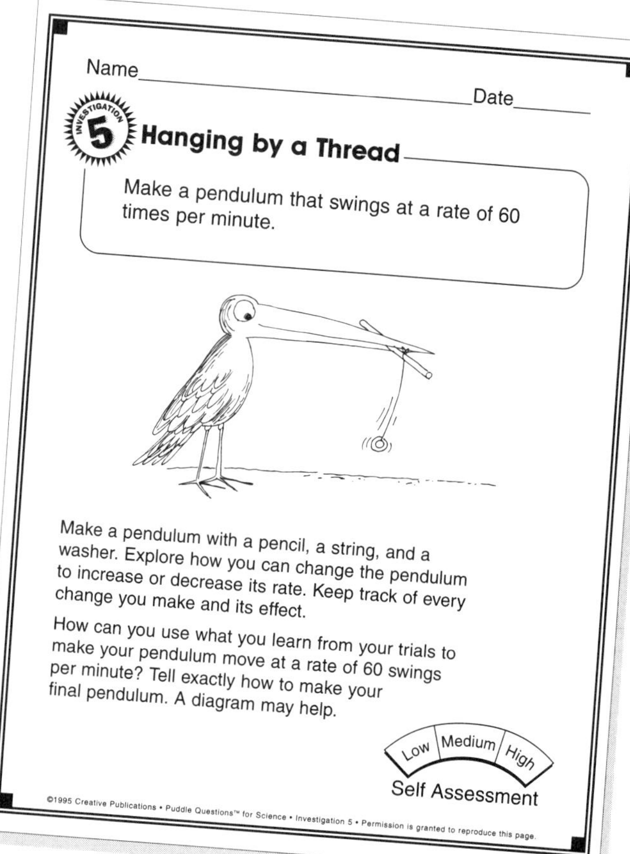

Name____________________ Date________

Hanging by a Thread

Make a pendulum that swings at a rate of 60 times per minute.

Make a pendulum with a pencil, a string, and a washer. Explore how you can change the pendulum to increase or decrease its rate. Keep track of every change you make and its effect.

How can you use what you learn from your trials to make your pendulum move at a rate of 60 swings per minute? Tell exactly how to make your final pendulum. A diagram may help.

Low / Medium / High

Self Assessment

©1995 Creative Publications • Puddle Questions™ for Science • Investigation 5 • Permission is granted to reproduce this page.

Blackline Master in English, page 85
and in Spanish, page 86

Science Processes

- Identifying potentially relevant factors
- Controlling variables
- Refining designs based on trial-and-error tests

Tools and Equipment

- ◆ different types of string
- ◆ metal washers of various weights and sizes
- ◆ rulers
- ◆ clocks or stopwatches
- ◆ blank paper
- ◆ lined writing paper
- ◆ pencils

Grouping Arrangement

Pairs or small groups

Time Frame

About an hour

Presenting the Investigation

1. Distribute a copy of the investigation to each student. Show the students how to make a pendulum using a string tied around a pencil and a metal washer for a bob. Release the bob from about a 30-degree angle to demonstrate how the pendulum should swing freely back and forth.
2. **Think about the factors that might influence the rate at which a pendulum swings. Explore with your pendulum. Try to make one that swings at a rate of 60 times per minute. You may change anything about your pendulum that you think could help you reach your target rate.**
3. Left on their own, students will come up with different definitions of a pendulum's swing. Some will define it as the distance from one side of the swing to the other, while others will think of it as beginning at one side of the swing and returning back to that point. For purposes of this investigation, as long as each group is consistent from trial to trial, the definition doesn't matter. However, rather than letting students come up with their own definitions, you may choose to establish that the definition is one swing back-and-forth.
4. As students work, they should record what changes they make, and the effect on their pendulum swing. Once students have achieved the desired results, they should use words and diagrams to convey exactly how to make their pendulum.

Assessment Criteria

It is important to let students know what they will be evaluated on in this assessment. Tell them that you are interested in finding out

- ✔ **how they experiment with the materials and potentially relevant factors**
- ✔ **how reliable their experimental procedures are**
- ✔ **whether their final pendulum actually swings at a rate of 60 times per minute**

Prompts for Getting Started

As students work, you might want to ask individuals questions such as these:

- **How many times does your pendulum swing in a minute? Do you need it to swing faster or slower?**
- **What could you do to your pendulum to get it to swing faster (or slower)?**
- **What are all the factors that *might* have an effect? How could you find out if each of those factors *does* have an effect?**

Assessing the Work

This is an assessment of students' abilities to analyze a problem, test the factors that they think might be relevant, and use what they learn from their experimentation to achieve a final, specified result. Some students will approach the challenge in a more systematic manner than others, using the results of previous trials to determine each subsequent action. Your observations of the students as they work, in combination with the students' reports and final pendulums, will be of value as you assess their success with this investigation. You will want to test the final pendulums to see if they actually swing at the target rate.

Questions to ask yourself while scoring a response:

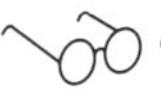

- **Are the testing methods used by the student reliable? Is the pendulum allowed to swing freely? Is the method of timing precise?**
- **Is a systematic approach taken to explore potentially relevant factors? Did the student use the results of previous trials to refine the pendulum?**
- **Did the student test only one factor at a time?**
- **Does the final pendulum swing at the target rate?**

Scoring Rubric

Low Response
No effort has been made to examine potentially relevant factors. Because of significantly faulty or haphazard testing, the student may feel that he or she has been successful; but upon examination, the final pendulum swings at a rate significantly different from 60 swings per minute.

Medium Response
An effort has been made to work with potentially relevant factors, although the student may not have used a systematic approach to the problem. Testing procedures may have been slightly flawed so that, upon examination, the final pendulum only *approaches* a rate of 60 swings per minute.

High Response
A systematic approach has been used to produce a 60-swings-per-minute pendulum. Careful testing procedures make the student's results highly reliable. Upon examination, the final pendulum is found to swing at the target rate, plus or minus a few seconds.

Pendulum Lab

At first, we wrapped the string many times around the pen, until it became very short. We then tied on the washer, and started time the swings. At first, a swing was one sway, but after many unsuccessful attemps, we concluded that one sway was too few, because we continued to get too many swings. We then lengthened the string, and began one swing as two sways. After this, we again counted the swings in a minute, but again up short. Once again, we shortened the length of the string, and timed the swings again. This didn't work, so for the next few minutes, we constantly lengthened and shortened the string, coming up long or short by only a few swings. After a while, we finally got 61 swings in a minute, our best results yet. For this final result, our string was 8 3/4 inches* from the pen to the washer and wrapped ten times around a pen. We considered a swing two sways or going one direction and back.

10 wraps
PEN
string 8 3/4 inches
washer
1 swing

High Response

When they found that their first pendulums swung much too quickly, this student and her partners decided to revise their definition of *swing* from "one side-to-side swing" to "one back-and-forth swing." Thereafter, the group used the results of each trial to lengthen or shorten the string until they had zeroed in on the desired number of swings.

Pendulum Paragraph

For the pendulum, we started with a string length of approximately 3/4 of the full length. We timed one minute and came up with 82 swings.* We watched the other groups that had far shorter strings. They got numbers like 156 per minute. Mai and I came to the conclusion that it needed to be longer to accomplish the 60 swings per minute. We lengthened the string to its full length. That came up with 75 swings per min. We tied two strings together and got a length of 109.5 cm. We then got 60 swings in 60 seconds.

* One swing equals one backwards or forwards — not both.

High Response

This student and her partner compare their first trial results with those of other groups. Since their pendulum already swings too fast, and the shorter pendulums of groups nearby swing even faster, they reason that they should lengthen their pendulum rather than shorten it.

Start with two feet 5 inches String. When you tie the String to the pen and the 1/4' wieght the String is one foot and ten inches long
we chang the weight to th 1/2" weight
It was off by a caple of seconds

We changed the String to kite line. To Six feet 5 inches. The weight stays the same. 5 feet Sever inches with pen and weight. Change String to 4 feet ten inches. Change to 2 feet six and a half inches

An inch below parralel in dropping it. Length is 3 feet one inch. The weight is 1/2" inch washer. The pen was 5 inches long without the cap. The Origanal length was six feet long. It worked an event 60 swings in a minute. Scince there was extra string we wand the extra around the pen. We used kite twine.

pen

String is 3 feet 1 inch

Kite twine

washer is 1/2" inch weight

Medium Response

The first pendulum produced by this student only misses the 60-swings-per-minute mark by a few seconds. Rather than making a small change to his pendulum to perfect it, he begins a series of random changes, including significantly increasing the string's length. He finally reaches the desired result, more through luck and flawed testing procedures than through a logical, systematic process.

Science

(We are counting a swing from the middle to the side)

Our first trial we swung and it went over sixty to 80 in one minute. Now we're going to shorten it.

For our second trial we shortened the rope and we messed up by shaking along with the rope and we endedup with 112!

For our third trial we didn't mess up and we shortened the rope and we got 63 in one minute.

for our fourth trial we added another string and a bigger washer and we got 60 swings in 1 minute!

for our fith trial we are going to add another washer so now we have two washes and a really long string and we got 64 swings out of 60 seconds.

Medium Response

This student randomly shortens and lengthens the pendulum's string, at times achieving remarkably similar results with significantly different string lengths because of haphazard testing procedures. The student made no attempt to revise the pendulum based on results of previous trials.

Pengulim Paragraph

The first thin we tried was to swing the pengulim oposite parrallell with the pencil. The pengulim went to fast so we made the pengulim shorter by raping it around the pencil, but it went faster. We considered a swing as when the washe reach full hight each time. Next we tried swing it parralel to the pincil and be tween our fingers, but it didn't work. The next pengulim was our succesful one. We made the string longer and aded a paper clip. After 3 tries the pengulim made it at exactly one minute.

Medium Response

This student alternately changes either the height of the washer's starting point or the length of the string, but he never uses the results of one trial to refine the pendulum design. The final revision involves a longer string and a paper clip, and it requires three tries before the pendulum is finally finessed into a 60-swings-per-minute rate.

Low Response

This student measures one minute by counting "with his head" rather than using a clock. Instead of changing anything about his pendulum, he simply changes the rate at which he counts. By his third trial, he is able to successfully coordinate his counting to sixty with the swinging of the pendulum.

We first counted with our heads and which turned out alot, it was 71. Our second try we got a bigger number than our first, it was 151 it was either I counted to fast or Chris counted to slow. Our third time I knew we were going to get something close and we got 61 swings in one minute.

A swing is something that swing back and forth.

Extending the Learning

1. Have each group display their most successful pendulum. Compare the characteristics of each one, and discuss any ideas the students have about why there are discrepancies in the designs. **If these are all 60-swings-per-minute pendulums, why aren't they all the same?**
2. Invite the students to share the processes they went through to come up with their most successful models, and have them tell about the various factors they manipulated in order to vary the pendulum rate.

~~ Talking It Over ~~

What kinds of factors seemed to have an effect on your pendulum's rate?

~ How long the string was really made a difference. It seemed like you could slow your pendulum down by making the string longer.

~ The smaller washers made it go slower, too.

~ I don't think so. We tried all the sizes of washers, and it didn't make any difference.

~ If you pull the washer up higher, like parallel to the pencil, it will go faster.

~ We were really close, and then I stood on a chair on my tiptoes and it worked. I don't know why, though.

~ We had some confusing things happen, but then we figured out it was because we weren't holding our hands still while the pendulum was swinging.

~ Yeah. It was hard to hold the pencil still and level, but if you didn't, the results wouldn't be accurate. Finally we tried resting the pencil on the edge of the table and swinging the pendulum. That worked great.

Follow-Up Activity

1. As a class, brainstorm a list of all the factors that the students feel might have an effect on the rate at which a pendulum swings. **How can we find out the effect of any particular factor?** Elicit that the factor must be tested in isolation, with all the other factors controlled, or held constant. You may want to discuss other ways in which test results can be made more reliable, such as through multiple repetitions of each trial with an average taken of each, or controlling the pendulum's swing by resting the pencil on the edge of a table or desk.
2. Have small groups of students each select one factor to test. Once the experimentation period is over, have groups who studied the same factor get together to compare results. They should discuss and try to explain any discrepancies in their findings.
3. Meet as a class to share conclusions. Have groups who tested each factor report on whether or not they found that factor to affect the rate of the pendulum. Although students are likely to list a number of other unforeseen factors, you may be interested to know that the length of the pendulum does have an effect on the rate (the longer the pendulum, the slower the rate), whereas the amplitude of the swing and the weight of the bob (under controlled circumstances) should not.

Ramp Rally

In this investigation, ramps and marbles serve as a framework within which students explore an optimization problem. Students are asked to experiment with their ramps to find the slope that makes the marble travel farthest. Though simply stated, this problem provides a rich context in which students can apply a variety of scientific processes. It will be interesting to note how different students organize their search for the optimal slope, and how they decide when they've identified it. Also of interest are the ways they choose to organize and communicate their data and interpretations of "the shape of the data."

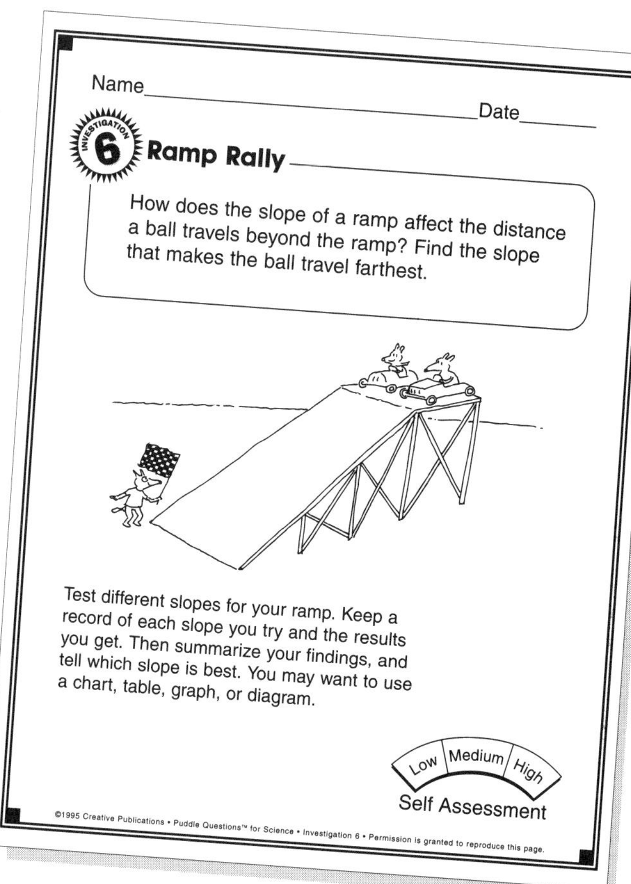
Name________________ Date________

Investigation 6 Ramp Rally

How does the slope of a ramp affect the distance a ball travels beyond the ramp? Find the slope that makes the ball travel farthest.

Test different slopes for your ramp. Keep a record of each slope you try and the results you get. Then summarize your findings, and tell which slope is best. You may want to use a chart, table, graph, or diagram.

Low / Medium / High
Self Assessment

©1995 Creative Publications • Puddle Questions™ for Science • Investigation 6 • Permission is granted to reproduce this page.

Blackline Master in English, page 87
and in Spanish, page 88

Science Processes

- Collecting data
- Interpreting experimental data
- Displaying data

Tools and Equipment

- paper towel tubes (cut in half lengthwise) or grooved rulers
- marbles
- measuring sticks or tapes
- blank paper
- lined writing paper
- graph paper
- pencils

Grouping Arrangement

Individuals or small groups

Time Frame

$1\frac{1}{2}$ to 2 hours

Presenting the Investigation

1. Show the students a marble and the "ramp" you have constructed by cutting a paper towel tube in half lengthwise. (If grooved rulers are available, students may opt to use those as ramps instead.) **How do you think the slope of a ramp affects the distance the marble travels? What if you wanted to find the slope that resulted in maximum roll distance?**
2. Have the students experiment with ramps and marbles to determine the optimal slope. Students will find different ways to set up their ramps to make different slopes. Some may use piles of books or stacks of paper. Others may measure the height they want to try, and then hold the end of their ramp at that level.
3. As the students work, observe and note the different approaches and experimental procedures they use. You may notice, for instance, that some students take a random approach to trying different ramp heights, while others are very deliberate, changing the ramp height by the same amount for each successive trial.
4. After completing the exploration and data-gathering phase of the investigation, students may organize their data in some way to show the information more clearly and write a summary of their findings and conclusions.

Assessment Criteria

It is important to let students know what they will be evaluated on in this assessment. Tell them that you are interested in finding out

- ✔ **how well organized, precise, and reliable their experimental procedures are**
- ✔ **what visual method they use to record and display their data**
- ✔ **how clearly and completely they communicate their findings**

Prompts for Getting Started

As students work, you may wish to ask questions such as these:

- **How can you test to see what slope makes the ball travel farthest? How can you keep track of the data you collect?**
- **What slope do you think is going to make the ball travel farthest?**
- **How can you describe or show the different slopes you are trying?**
- **How can you show your results clearly?**

Assessing the Work

In this assessment, we are interested in finding out how students go about solving an optimization problem. Precision, reliability, and organization of the experimental procedures are all important aspects to look at. In addition, this problem presents a perfect opportunity for students to make use of graphs, charts, or diagrams to organize and display their experimental data. Your observations of students as they work will be an important tool as you assess their work on this investigation.

Questions to ask yourself while scoring a response:

- **Did the student take care to conduct a well-organized and reliable experiment?**
- **Did the student measure precisely?**
- **Are the experimental data presented in a clear and logical manner?**
- **How clear is the explanation of the student's findings and conclusions?**

Scoring Rubric

Low Response
No conscious effort was applied to organizing a systematic search for optimal ramp height, and the student may only have tested a few different ramp heights before concluding which was optimal. The response is extremely vague in terms of relating experimental data, results, and conclusions.

Medium Response
Data have been gathered in a systematic manner and are clearly conveyed through the use of a chart or graph. The response may include an explanation for the data presented.

High Response
A significant amount of data has been gathered in a systematic manner, and a conscious effort has been made to make the data reliable. The data display method chosen is effective, and data may be presented in more than one way. The student uses the data to draw logical conclusions about the trends noted in roll distance as related to ramp height.

NOTES

H = height in inches of angle
F = marble rolling distance or how Far

1. Trial	2. Trial
0 inch H, 0 inches F	0 inch H, .5 inches F
1 inch H, 11 inches F	1 inches H, 15.5 inches F
2 inch H, 28 inches F	2 inches H, 24 inches F
3 inch H, 43 inches F	3 inches H, 41 inches F
4 inch H, 48 inches F	4 inches H, 48.5 inches F
5 inch H, 53 inches F	5 inches H, 53 inches F
6 inch H, 65.5 inches F	6 inches H, 63.5 inches F
7 inch H, 76.5 inches F	7 inches H, 70 inches F
8 inch H, 75.5 inches F	8 inches H, 69 inches F
9 inch H, 48.5 inches F	9 inches H, 51 inches F
10 inch H, 48 inches F	10 inches H, 50 inches F
11 inch H, 37 inches F	11 inches H, 36 inches F
12 inch H, 5 inches F	12 inches H, 8 inches F

AVERAGES

0" H, 0.25" F
1" H, 13.25" F
2" H, 26" F
3" H, 42" F
4" H, 42.25" F
5" H, 53" F
6" H, 64.5" F
7" H, 73.25" F
8" H, 72.25" F
9" H, 49.75" F
10" H, 49" F
11" H, 28.5" F
12" H, 6.5" F

0" = 0°
1" = 5°

High Response

This response is exceptional. For each slope, the group ran two trials and averaged the results to provide more reliable data. The student's graph provides a powerful visual image of the shape of their data, using an appropriate scale, and including exact roll distance measurements as well. A meticulous summary of procedures is given, with findings clearly stated. Optimal ramp height figures have also been translated into angle measures for added clarity.

Summary

We taped one ruler onto a straight side of a box, and propped a 12 inch ruler from 0" to the floor. We rolled the marble down it, and measured the distance that the marble rolled from the end of the ruler to where the marble lay. We did this for inches 0 – 12, re-propping the ruler each time. I took the information in a sort of ratio: the height that the 12 inch ruler starts being propped from (the hypotenuse) (H) : (F) the distance that the marble traveled. The higher the hypotenuse starting, the steeper the ramp. Taking these kind of notes, we did two trials, then averaged the marble travel distance. The ramp with the 7" H had the lagest Distance -- 73.25 inches. I also made a graph showing the marble distance relative to the slope.

The extremes, 0 and 12, didn't work very well. 0 hardley moved and 12 bounced.

7 inches is the hight at witch the slope works best. The angle at 7 inches is 35°.

High Response

After running her trials at 1-inch intervals and logging the information, this student reorganizes her data in an unusual way, sorting from shortest to longest distance. She then takes the extra step of checking the roll distances between 7 inches and 8 inches to refine her best slope data. The conclusions she draws given her experimental data are logical and clear.

The best slope angle is about 41.6° wich is a height of 7 3/4 inches and a length of 9 inches. The slope as it increaces in height makes the marble go farther untill it reaches 7 3/4 inches its peak and then starts to decrese. We think that is because the impact of the marble hitting the ground at such a steep slope slows it down.

height	how far the marble rolled
1 inch =	68 in.
2 inch =	84.5 in.
3 inch =	91.5 in.
11 inch =	105 in.
4 inch =	115.5 in.
9 inch =	115.5 in.
5 inch =	119 in.
10 inch =	122 in.
6 inch =	129 in.
7 inch =	133 in.
8 inch =	140 in.

7 1/2 inch = 139 in.

* 7 3/4 inch = 142 in. *

~~1cm = 1inch~~

H	D
1.) 1cm =	23.5 inch
2.) 1inch =	26 inches
3.) 1.5in =	29 inches
4.) 2inch =	3ft.
5.) 2.5in	44.5 in
6.) 3 in.	4ft 6in
7.) 3.5 in.	58 in.
8.) 4 in.	5'4"
9.) 5 in	5'4"
10.) 4.5 in	68.5
11.) 5 in	70
12.) 5.5 in	70
13.) 6 in	72 in.
14.) 6.5	70 in
15.) 7	61 in.
16.) 7.5	64 in.
17.) 8	57 in.
18.) 8.5	56.5
19.) 9 in	57 in.
20.) 9.5	36 in.
21.) 10	41 in.
22.) 10.5	26.5
23.) 11	22
24.) 11.5	15.5
25.) 12	13

the slope of six inches makes the marble go the farthest becaause it gives the marble momentom and the slant change from the ramp to the rug

Medium Response

This student runs twenty-five trials, increasing the ramp height of each successive trial by half an inch. He then states the optimal ramp height and gives a plausible explanation of his findings.

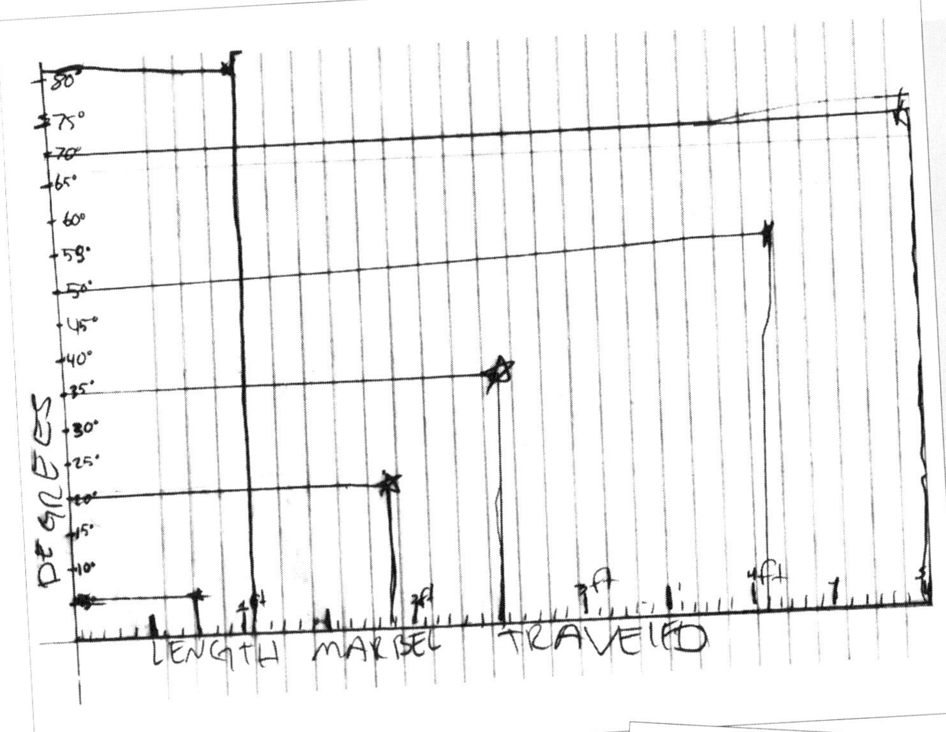

Medium Response

The graph constructed by this student is an effective means of communicating the results of her group's trials. They have taken the initiative to collect their data in terms of angle measures, but have run just six trials before deciding on an optimal slope.

Low Response

This student runs just three trials in order to identify the optimal slope. Although he does record the distance the marble traveled in each trial, he doesn't specify the ramp heights they resulted from. He finds a relationship between ramp height and distance traveled, but had he run more trials, he would have realized that this relationship shifts after a certain slope.

DIAGRAM:

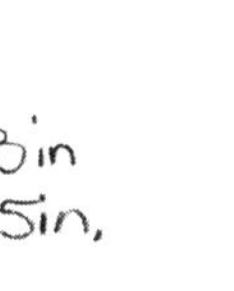

My findings were that the lower the angle the farther the marble would travel. My farthest travel made by the marble was 5feet 5inches!

Extending the Learning

1. Ask each student or cooperative group to share the slope or ramp height they found to be optimal, and record the slopes on the chalkboard. Ask why they think different groups came up with different results. The care with which measurements were taken, what type of ramp was used, and how the marble was released are all ideas that might be discussed. This may also be a good opportunity to discuss the concept of experimental reliability. Some students may have noticed that the same slope doesn't always yield exactly the same roll distance. Ask the students if they have any ideas about how they could have made their experimental data more reliable.
2. Ask the students how they actually found the optimal slope. Have different students explain their procedures. Have them share their ideas about the relationship between slope and roll distance.
3. Pairs of students may get together, exchange reports, and give feedback on the effectiveness of the display method (chart, graph, etc.). **Are the data clear? Can you tell what the optimal slope is? Can you see what the trends are as the ramp slope changes?**

~~ Talking It Over ~~

What did you find out about how slope and roll distance are related?

~ The steeper the ramp, the farther the marble goes.

~ No. That's only true up to a certain point. If the ramp is too steep, the marble hits the floor too hard and doesn't roll as far.

How did you know for sure you'd found the slope that maximized roll distance?

~ We tried about five different slants, and one was a lot better than the others, so we knew we found the best. We got lucky right away.

~ Well, you don't really know you found the best if you only tried a few. We tried every height from zero to twelve inches. Eight worked the best. Since we tried them all, we know we found the best one.

~ Okay, but I tried every half inch. You might have missed a better slope in between two inches.

~ The same height turns out different sometimes, so we double-checked. We did two rolls for every ramp height and took the average.

Follow-Up Activity

1. Stage a ramp rally in your classroom. Invite the students to set up their ramps according to the optimal slopes (or heights) they identified during their experimentation. Everyone sends one marble down their ramp and measures the distance. Whoever has the marble that goes the farthest is the winner.
2. Discuss as a class the results of the rally. Make a list of the different slopes set up by each student or group, and the distance their marble traveled. **Did your marbles travel the same distance this time that they did when you initially gathered your data? Was the winning ramp the only one set up for that particular slope? What if we did it again? Do you think the same ramp would win? Why or why not?** Discuss the various factors that might cause discrepancies.
3. Ask the students to define a set of rules for the rally that would improve reliability. Give them ten minutes or so to experiment with their ramps and marbles in an attempt to improve their distance. Some students might try slopes at intervals that they didn't try before. Others may perform multiple trials at the same ramp slope.
4. Hold another ramp rally using the "new and improved" ramp slopes and following the rally rules outlined by the students.

Ice Insulation

Here, students will design an experiment to test their ideas about what keeps an ice cube from melting. Students must figure out how to set up the experiment so they can monitor the results throughout the day. How will they know when an ice cube has melted if it is packed in a tight container? Students who switch classes during the day may also need to think about how they can transport their experiments in order to keep a close watch.

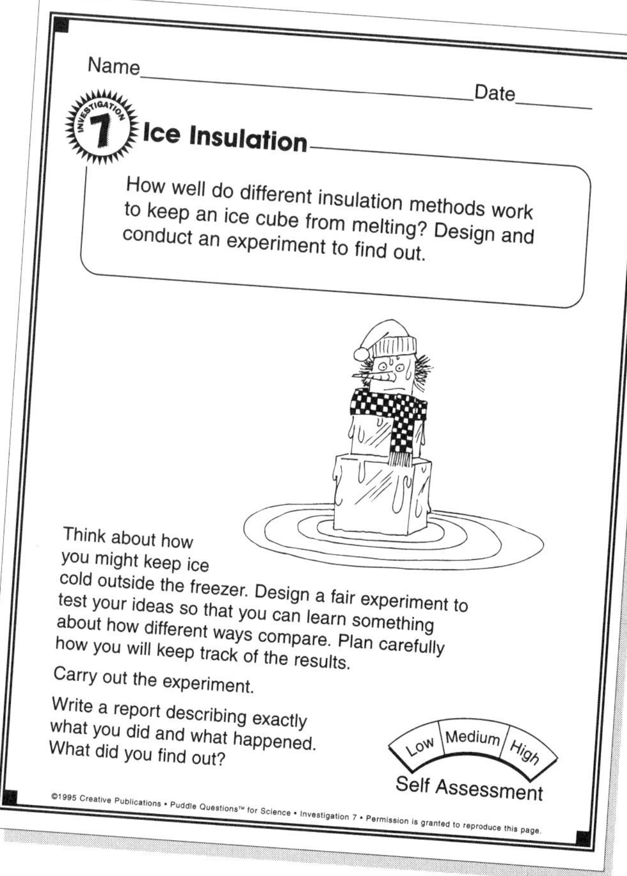

Name______________________________ Date________

Ice Insulation

How well do different insulation methods work to keep an ice cube from melting? Design and conduct an experiment to find out.

Think about how you might keep ice cold outside the freezer. Design a fair experiment to test your ideas so that you can learn something about how different ways compare. Plan carefully how you will keep track of the results.

Carry out the experiment.

Write a report describing exactly what you did and what happened. What did you find out?

Low Medium High

Self Assessment

©1995 Creative Publications • Puddle Questions™ for Science • Investigation 7 • Permission is granted to reproduce this page.

Blackline Master in English, page 89
and in Spanish, page 90

Science Processes

- Designing and conducting an experiment
- Comparing results
- Drawing conclusions

Tools and Equipment

- ice cubes in a cooler
- tape
- scissors
- miscellaneous materials (see Presenting the Investigation)
- blank paper
- lined writing paper
- pencils

Grouping Arrangement

Pairs or small groups

Time Frame

About an hour for setting up the experiments

Brief periods during the day to monitor experiments

30–60 minutes for writing reports

Presenting the Investigation

1. Show the class an ice cube from the cooler. **Suppose you want to keep an ice cube from melting for as long as possible out of a freezer. Design an experiment to compare different insulation methods so you'll know what works and what doesn't.** Point out the cooler and the materials you have gathered (a variety of fabrics, salt, sand, foil, plastic wrap, sawdust, waxed paper, plastic cups, plastic foam containers, packing materials, newspaper, paper towels, etc.).
2. Tell the students that you will be holding an Ice Insulation Contest as a follow-up to this assessment. For now their task is to design an experiment so that they can learn how different insulation methods compare, *not* to come up with the very best way. All groups will share what they learn, so everyone can use the information for the contest.
3. Have students plan and carry out their experiments. Warn them that they will need to check on their ice cubes throughout the day. They must be sure to set up their experiments so they can monitor what happens. **Be sure to take notes so you'll remember exactly what you did and what happened.**
4. After the ice cubes have melted, have the students complete their reports, recording descriptions of each insulator they tested and noting any conclusions they drew.

Assessment Criteria

It is important to let students know what they will be evaluated on in this assessment. Tell them that you are interested in finding out

- ✔ **whether the experiment they set up is a fair comparison of different methods**
- ✔ **how clearly and precisely they record their procedures and findings**
- ✔ **what conclusions they are able to draw**

Tell the students that they will *not* be evaluated on

- ✔ **whether their methods actually work better than other students' ways**

Prompts for Getting Started

If students have difficulty thinking of an experimental test, you might ask questions such as the following:

- **What is one method you think might work to keep ice cold? Can you think of another method to use as a comparison?**
- **What do you hope to find out from your experiment? Will your experiment give you the answers you are looking for?**

Assessing the Work

With this assessment question, we take a look at how students are able to set up and monitor experiments and whether the conclusions they draw from their experimental results can be reasonably inferred from the data. It's a window into students' understanding of what an experiment is and what can be learned from it. Some will set up highly controlled experiments, while others will compare two or more very different methods with no attempt at controlling variables. Your observations of the procedures students follow in setting up their experiments will be important in determining whether they understand the importance of controlling variables in scientific experimentation.

Questions to ask yourself while scoring a response:

- **Is the experiment a fair test of the methods compared?**
- **What procedures were used? Was an attempt made to control variables?**
- **Did the student keep careful records of procedures and results?**
- **What, if any, conclusions were drawn? Can they be reasonably drawn from the experimental data and results?**

Scoring Rubric

Low Response
Only one insulation method may have been tested, and relatively little information is given about the results. Conclusions, if given, may be based on faulty reasoning.

Medium Response
Two or more insulation methods are tested and compared, but little attempt is made to control variables. Elapsed-time comparisons are documented, although possibly not with great precision, and results for the different methods are compared. Conclusions, if given, may not be justified.

High Response
A controlled experiment was set up to compare two or more insulation methods. Care was taken to make the test fair. For example, the student may have made sure that the amounts of materials used were comparable. Elapsed-time comparisons are documented with precision, and results for the different methods are compared. A reasonable conclusion is drawn.

What well keep an ice cube from not melting? I well conduct an experiment to find out. I used paper plates, styrofoam, and an ice cube for each one. I put salt, sawdust, and sand each in a seperate plate. I had the ice cube on the plate and covered one with salt, another with sawdust and the third one with sand. I covered each one with a styrofoam cup

top view

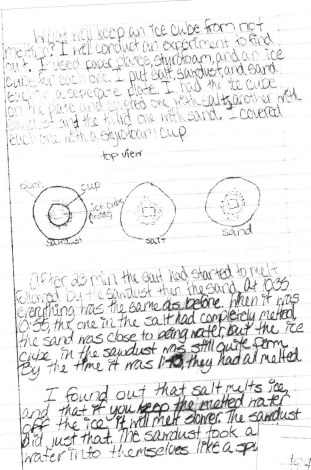

plate
cup
ice cube (inside)
sawdust
salt
sand

After 23 min the salt had started to melt followed by the sawdust then the sand. At 10:35 everything was the same as before. When it was 10:55, the one in the salt had completely melted, the sand was close to being water, but the ice cube in the sawdust was still quite ferm. By the time it was 1:10, they had all melted.

I found out that salt melts ice, and that if you keep the melted water off the ice, it will melt slower. The sawdust did just that. The sawdust took a[...] water into themselves like a spo[...]

High Response

In this experiment, three different insulating materials—sawdust, salt, and sand—are compared and rated. The sawdust turned out to be the best ice insulator, followed by the sand and then the salt. A possible reason for the results comes from the observation that the sawdust actually soaks up the melted water like a sponge. The student speculates that keeping the melted water off the ice cube may help it stay frozen longer.

Here is how you put my experament together. First you take two cups and put the tops together. Than you tape one long piece of tape and tape together the two cups. Next you take sissors and poke a hole in one styrofome cup and cut three lines to make a door. Now comes the ice cube. You wrap the ice cube in foil. Finally, you put the ice cube into the door. Repeat the same thing with the other two cups, but wrap the ice cube in saran wrap. At the end, your cup should look like this.

What happens? The first half hour after I checked it the ice cube in the saran-wrap was already starting to melt! I checked the other door. The ice cube in the tin-foil was not melting! The first time I checked the cups it was

This time I checked the cups the saran-wraped ice cube was half melted. The tinfoil was still not melting! Of corse, this time it is 10:05.

Finally, it is 11:45. The saran wrap is 3 quarters melted!!! The tin foil is now about 1 quarter melted!

The next time I checked my project it was melted!!! I've really learned something from my project, though. I've learned that tinfoil helps ice cubes last longer. Saran wrap is not very good at it, though. I experimented with saranwrap and tinfoil because I've seen people wrap tinfoil around drinking bottles to keep it cold. I experienced with saran wrap to see if it works as well as tin foil. (It didn't!!!)

High Response

This student has an ingenious way of setting up his experiment so that he can easily monitor the results over time without dismantling the two ice insulators each time he checks on his ice cubes. His conclusion that foil is a better insulator than plastic wrap is supported by his results.

Medium Response

Here, two completely different methods of insulating ice are tested and compared. The student zeroes in on the play dough and its salt content as the critical element that made her second method last longer than her first, a conclusion that cannot be deduced from her experiment since so many other other uncontrolled factors are involved.

Ice insulation expirament

This morning, instead of doing reading, we did something more exciting. We did an expirament on ice insulators these are Rebeca and my ~~my~~ expiraments:

Supplies: Styrophone bowl
Wax paper
Salt
Plastic cup
Small ice cubes
Tape

bowl w/ small ice cubes covered wax
cup w/ ice cubes + salt

Started: 9:35 Melted: 10:15 ≈

We first put ice into the plastic cup with the salt. traced the wax paper on the cup top, and filled the bowl with ice cubes. Between the bowl and the cup, we put wax. In the traced circle, we ~~waited~~ poked holes into it. Cold air + cold water would trinkle down to main cube making it cool. This didn't work very well because the wax paper broke, and all of the ice fell to the bottom cup.

Supplies: plastic cup
ice cubes
sawdust
bubble paper
sand
play dough
foil
rubber band

bubble paper foil rubber band
in cup sawdust sand playdough, ice cube

Started: 9:36 Melted: 1:30

This ~~one~~ expirament was more expiramental, but it sure did last longer than the other one. First, we put sawdust and sand on bottom of cup. Then we put bubblepaper inside the cup, but taped it outside to make a swing for the ice. We then covered the ice w/ playdough because playdough is mainly made out of ~~mainly~~ salt. We foiled it, rubber banded it and poked holes on top for ~~it~~ the ice to breath the cold air around us ~~dough~~.

The second one was better probably because of the playdough. The playdough kept the ice cool on the inside. I found out that salt helps in any form: playdough, plain salt, rock salt anything!

I am going to conduct an experiment will tell me if sawdust and styrafoam is a better or worse insulator for ice. At 9:15am I put sawdust an ice cube into an air tight ziplock bag. Next I put it in a styraphome cup with ice. After that I taped another styraphome cup on top.

In my next experiment I took a bowl and put an ice cube covered with sand. Finally I put it in the dark. The time is 9:20am. I think sawdust will work.

PLEASE TURN OVES

11:00am - Oh no! The ice covered with sand is gone! One good thing is there is more than 3/4 of the other ice cube left.

5:30pm - The one in the sawdust is gone now! It has been 8 hours and fifteen minutes. At least one exp-rement worked! This experiment is worth while because if I don't have a freezer I can still store ice!

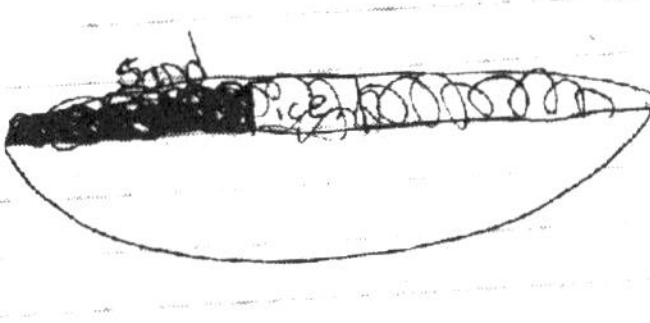

Medium Response

This student set out to learn whether sawdust or plastic foam was the better insulator, but the packaging and placement (one is placed in the dark) of the two insulator ideas are completely different, making it impossible to know which material works better. His report documents his observations at two times during the day, but the melting time for each method is not clearly stated.

I put a ice cube in a cup. Inside the cup it was wraped with foil. I put a ice cube inside it. We use a piece of aluminum and put it inside the cup and put an ice cube on it. It didn't last very long. It was fun to do it and I like to do it sometime again. It lasted more than two hours. We used some tape to stick the aluminum and it didn't leak.

Low Response

Only one method for insulating an ice cube is tested in this response, and data on its melting rate are not given precisely in the report. No comparison is made with other methods.

Extending the Learning

1. Gather the class together to share their work. Let each pair or cooperative group explain their experiment and what they found out. They can show the insulating methods they investigated, making it clear to the class how they set up their experiments.
2. As each report is presented, have the class critique the methods used. Talk about what each group is trying to test and how they might improve their experimental procedures to ensure a fair test of the methods selected. Write any generalizations or conclusions on the chalkboard (for example, foil works better than plastic wrap, or draining off the water makes the ice cube last longer).

~~ Talking It Over ~~

What were some problems you had in doing your experiments?

~ I thought that an airtight package would keep the ice coldest. But we had to check the ice cube every so often so I couldn't make it work. Because if I took the tape off all the cold air would escape and the warm air would melt the ice cube.

~ I don't think we were as careful as we could have been. We may have done things slightly differently on certain cups. In order to be sure of which worked better, all of the cups should have been constructed exactly the same.

~ I used salt to suck up all the water that melted, then I waited 20 minutes. It didn't work very well, but I think if I put more salt in every 10 minutes the ice would have stayed frozen longer.

~ We put some ice cubes in a cup and then we set another ice cube on some wax paper above them. But when we checked it after 40 minutes, it had collapsed. The wax paper was too thin to support it. Soon all the cubes froze together into one big chunk, including our main ice cube, and that was the end of that!

What did you learn from your experiment?

~ My prediction was that foil would keep the ice cube cold, but I was wrong. The bubble packing stuff worked the best. But I don't know why.

~ I learned that you don't have to have a freezer to keep things cold.

Follow-Up Activity

1. Hold an Ice Insulation Contest in your classroom. Using what they learned from their own experiments and those of their classmates, students should think about how they could combine the best methods to make an ice insulator that will last the longest. Have each pair or small group make just one insulator to enter into the contest.
2. Have the students decide as a class how they will monitor the cubes to see which one melts last. The students, by now, should have enough experience with melting time frames to make some fairly accurate assumptions about how soon and how often they'll need to be checking the cubes. When everyone is ready, give each group an ice cube. The ice cubes should be placed in the ice-saving models simultaneously. Note the starting time on the chalkboard.
3. Some students may be interested in organizing a chart to keep track of the elapsed times for all of the models. The class could then analyze any common features of the most successful models.

Practice Makes Perfect

In this investigation, students are asked to think of some skill or activity that might improve with practice and to design an experiment that would help them find out if their assumption is correct. The topics of interest to students will vary widely, from speed reading to "yo-yoing" to juggling. The abilities of the students to think through and describe an appropriate experiment will vary as well, and this forms the heart of the challenge. Some students will simply outline an experiment, while others will diligently think through the experiment in detail and address all of the stumbling blocks that they detect.

Name______________________________ Date________

8 Practice Makes Perfect

Think of something that you suspect might improve with practice. Design an experiment to find out if it does improve.

Tell what you want to find out. Think about different ways you could design an experiment to help you find out.

Describe the experiment you think would work best and tell why. Explain exactly how to set up your experiment so that someone else can do it.

Low Medium High
Self Assessment

©1995 Creative Publications • Puddle Questions™ for Science • Investigation 8 • Permission is granted to reproduce this page.

Blackline Master in English, page 91
and in Spanish, page 92

Science Processes

- Identifying experimental questions
- Designing experiments

Tools and Equipment

- blank paper
- lined writing paper
- pencils

Grouping Arrangement

Individuals

Time Frame

1–1½ hours

Presenting the Investigation

1. **What are some skills that you think might improve with practice? Think of things that you could actually test through an experiment, then choose one of your ideas and design an experiment to help you determine the effect of practice.** Make sure the students understand that they won't actually be *conducting* their experiments as part of this investigation, but that you're interested to see how successful they are in *designing* experiments to reliably test a particular question.
2. Students should spend some time thinking about and evaluating different topics for their experiments. Some of their ideas will lend themselves to experimentation, while others may not. Students should pick the idea that they feel will provide the strongest and most interesting experimental situation.
3. Once students have chosen an idea to test through experimentation, have them think through their experiments—what the experimental procedures should be, the equipment needed, how to set up and monitor the experiment, the time required, and so on. Tell the students that it might help to imagine themselves actually doing their experiments from start to finish. They'll be more apt to write complete summaries of their experiments, since they'll have thought about important details and possible problems ahead of time.
4. Once students have thought through their experiments, they should write down their ideas in as complete and detailed a form as possible.

Assessment Criteria

It is important to let students know what they will be evaluated on in this assessment. Tell them that you are interested in finding out

- ✔ **whether the idea they have chosen to test truly lends itself to experimentation**
- ✔ **whether the experiment they design is a logical and fair way to test their question**
- ✔ **how clear, complete, and detailed the description of their experiment is**

Prompts for Getting Started

Questions like these may help students get started:

- **Have you thought of a skill that might improve with practice? What is it?**
- **What kind of experiment could you do to test the effect of practice on that skill?**
- **How could you tell if practice makes a difference?**

Assessing the Work

In this assessment, we look at students' abilities to design experiments to answer particular questions. The challenge of the investigation is to find a topic or question that can be tested through experimentation, then to design an experiment that would be a logical test of that question. Although most sixth-grade students should be able to identify testable questions, the level of detail they provide about the experimental procedures is likely to vary widely.

Questions to ask yourself while scoring a response:

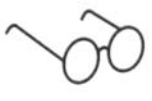

- **Is the student able to identify a question that can be tested through experimentation?**
- **Has the student devised a logical and fair way to test the question?**
- **Has the student thought through and described the experiment and its procedures in detail?**

Scoring Rubric

Low Response
A question has been identified, although the experimental procedures, as described, are very sketchy and may not be a logical test of the question. No plans for measuring improvement are proposed.

Medium Response
A question has been selected, and a logical experiment to test it has been proposed. The description of the experimental procedures may lack detail, but the experiment is definitely workable.

High Response
A question has been selected, and a logical experiment to test it has been proposed. The experiment has been planned in detail, and the explanation clearly relates the procedures.

In the experiment How Long can You Balance a Book on your Head? We tried to measure if practice would improve the skill of moving with a book on your head. We set up a chart that will incorporate 10 trials of walking around with a book on your head. The experiment should be done with three peope, which we did. While conducting the experiment the participants should walk at a pace of 5 steps per 7 seconds, and continually walk around obstacles, drink from drinking fountains climb ladders and more. Short periods of sitting down are acceptable also. Our averaged results fluxtuated, but gradually grew better. We decided to use averages to get the most normal answer possible. One downfall of our experiment, is that we didn't always take the same route. Some-times there was more danger of losing the book tran at others. The experiment that would work better would be sitting still the whole time.

The book is 15 cm. by 22cm. by 3cm.
The book weighs 80 grams

We are walking around at a pace of about 5 steps every 7 sec.
We are also stepping on top and around of various areas.
How long you can balance a book on your head?

	1	2	3	4	5	6	7	8	9	10
Person 1	7 sec	30 sec	5 sec	25 sec	45 sec	30 sec	60 sec	45 sec	80 sec	80 sec
Person 2	75 sec	210 sec	285 sec	165 sec	15 sec	15 sec	60 sec	180 sec	225 sec	570 sec
Person 3	195 sec	240 sec	100 sec	180 sec	180 sec	75 sec	15 sec	170 sec	190 sec	75 sec
average	92 sec	160 sec	130 sec	123 sec	80 sec	40 sec	45 sec	131 sec	161 sec	241 sec

High Response

This response gives concrete data as the student couldn't resist carrying out an experiment on developing skill in balancing a book on the head. Along with a multitude of details, the student also notes one of the shortcomings of the experiment and suggests a less interesting adaptation that would ensure more controlled conditions.

I think an experiment that would work is "Do your muscles improve as you do something?" Something you can do is chin ups. What you would do is go out to a park or other place that has the appropiate bars. You should take a stop watch with you.

You'd probably need someone to help. You could an amount you want to do. Someone sets the watch on 0:00. Tell them to start the watch while you start on the chin ups. As soon as you finish the chin ups the other person stops the watch. Record the number done and how long it took to do them.

The next day go back. Try to do the same number. Repeat the steps before. Try to do them at the same time each day. That's because at different times in the day you'd feel different. Late at night you might be tired. After meals you shouldn't. If you do them at the same time the conditions will be about the same.

The further into the project the faster and eaiser you will be able to do them. Your muscles will have gotten stronger so you'll do better.

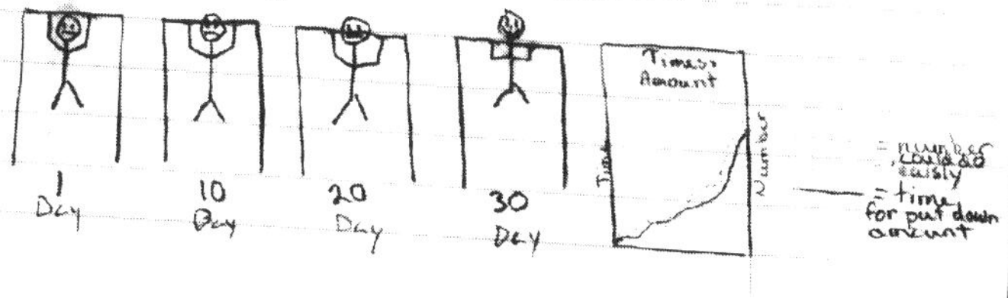

High Response

In his experiment to determine the effect of practice on muscle strength, this student notes that it would be helpful to have a friend available to operate the stopwatch. He also reasons that for test results to be most reliable, the chin-ups should be done at about the same time every day.

High Response

An effective experiment to measure the effect of practice on the skill of writing with the nondominant hand is outlined by this student. His detailed instructions for the setup and execution of the experiment make his thinking crystal clear.

Almost all the skills you have or are possible of having can improve with practice. For example writing with either hand you don't usually write with. You could test this by using your indominant hand to write the alphabet or one sentence over several times. You could write the alphabet or the sentence over as many times as you wanted,but if you were trying your writing would probably get better.

I would set it up like this:
The person testing would sit at a table with another person. The person testing would sit with there dominant hand on their lap or behind their back. First they would write the alphabet once while timing how long it took them to write it. When they were done with the alphabet they would look over what they wrote,they would count the number of mistakes then have the other person look it over.
After this exercise, the person testing would write one sentence ten times(with not dominant hand)every time timing how long it took them to write the sentence,counting the number of mistakes they made and having the other person critique it.The person critiquing it would say if it got better or stayed the same.
When done with the sentences the tester would write the alpha-bet again timing it,counting mistakes and having the other person critique it. The two people would then look over the results and see how it changed(NOTE:the tester may have to write the sentences more than ten times.)

DIRECTIONS:

1.Get a partner,a couple pieces of paper,a pencil and a watch.
2.While your partner is timing you write the alphabet with your not dominant hand.
3.Look over the alphabet that you wrote with your partner; record how long it took you to write the alphabet and count your mistakes(record mistakes, too).
4.Now write a sentence with your not dominant hand.Have your partner time you.Count the number of mistakes and have your partner critique what you wrote.Do this over ten or more times.Make sure to record any changes.
5.Write the alphabet again and look it over. Is anything different?

My expiriment is to see how long it takes me to lean how to talk normally (so people can understand the first time I say something)

Talk for one hour every day for a week. You should say words that are difficult for you. You should talk to youself at your home if passable. If you are still having trouble practice for another week and so on and so forth.

(The reason I did this is because I just got an apliance on my teeth)

Medium Response

A recent event in this student's life has prompted her to design an experiment to test the effect of practice on enunciation. Although she has chosen a testable question, she doesn't describe her experiment in detail, nor does she say how she would assess clarity or measure progress.

Drawing a picture.

I will draw the same thing over and over and see it it improves.

2.

3.

4.

5.

6.

Each one is different, but each one is nice.

Well, I can't think of any think of any other way to do this experiment or think of any other experiment.

Draw a picture.
Then draw it about 6 times.

Medium Response

This student's idea to test the effect of practice on drawing skill is an interesting one. Upon trying his experiment, however, he realizes that it's difficult to gauge improvement, and he is unable to think of a better way to conduct the experiment.

I can get better at basket ball, even though I don't usually play it. I practice basket ball because it's my favorite sport, and I want to learn how to play it.

Here are somethings that I would do to improve basketball:

A. Run 1 mile a day.
B. Try jump the highest that I can
C. Shoot the ball from far away
D. If didn't, move 1 feet to the hoop.
E. If did, move 1 feet back
F. Do that every day, don't skip 1 day!
G. Have fun!!

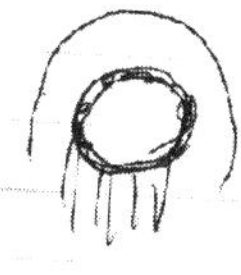

Low Response

Rather than describing an experiment that would help him assess the effect of practice on his basketball skills, this student offers a workout routine. He has not thought to identify a single measurable aspect of basketball to focus on, nor has he thought about how he would measure success.

Extending the Learning

1. Have the students pair up and read each other's work, imagining that they're actually going to do their partner's experiment. Students should evaluate their partner's work in terms of the following questions: **Does the report provide enough information about how the experiment should be set up and run? Is the description of the experiment complete? Are there any missing details?**
2. After partners have reviewed each other's reports, have them discuss their thoughts, asking questions about missing information, details not explained, or things that may not work as intended, and giving their partner suggestions for improving their experiment.
3. Bring the class together to discuss their work on this investigation. Topics such as how the students decided on questions for their experiments, what different experiments they considered, how they decided on the best experiment to test their question, and why they set their experiments up as they did are all interesting discussion sparkers.

~~ Talking It Over ~~

What things were important to consider as you designed your experiments?

~ You have to decide how to figure out if you're getting better.

~ My experiment was on tongue twisters. At first I didn't really think about how I could tell if I was getting better. Then I tried it a few times and decided I needed to time how long it took me to say it. Then I could see if I was getting faster.

~ But you could go faster and just be really slurring. Maybe you should also count how many mistakes you make, or have someone judge whether they can really hear each word.

What else were you thinking about as you devised your experiments?

~ You should say how many times the thing should be practiced. Otherwise, no one would know when the experiment was done.

~ In my violin experiment, I thought you shouldn't tell the person that you're testing them. If they're nervous about being in an experiment, they might make a lot of mistakes they wouldn't normally make.

Follow-Up Activity

1. As a follow-up to this investigation, have your students set up and conduct their experiments either at home or at school. The time frames involved in students' experiments are likely to vary widely, so be prepared for this phase of the investigation to go on for a week or so, depending on the experiments.
2. For many students, conducting their experiments will be a natural lead-in to a revision effort. They may find unanticipated factors that influence their results, and they may want to make corrections in their next effort. Also, as students set up and ran the experiments, they may have discovered details they had not thought through. Give the students a chance to revise their original experiment descriptions based on their experiences and on any suggestions resulting from the class discussion.

Blackline Masters

Student Pages

Each investigation has a student page in English and in Spanish (see pages 77–92). Photocopies of the pages can be made and distributed to each student or group of students. Alternatively, an overhead transparency can be made and displayed during work on each investigation.

Self Assessment pages 93, 94

Copies of these self-assessment sheets can be given to students after they have completed each investigation. The form is available in English and in Spanish. Students shade in the self-assessment dial to rate their performance and then record their reflections on their performance.

Observation Sheet page 95

These forms can be used to record observations of individual students as they work on the investigations.

Record Keeping page 96

Here is a place to record student scores on the eight investigations.

Name____Date__________

Puddle Observations

Describe a puddle in every way you can think of.

Find a puddle. Examine it closely. Record what you find out about your puddle.

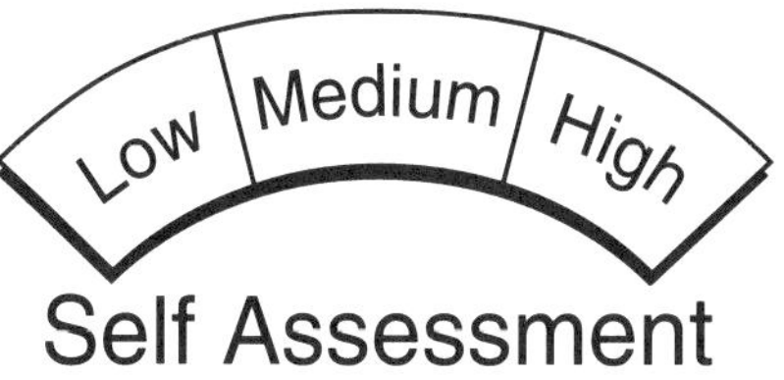

Self Assessment

Nombre________________________________Fecha__________

Observaciones de un charco

Describe un charco de tantas maneras como puedas.

Halla un charco. Examínalo detenidamente.
Luego anota tus observaciones del charco.

Evaluación propia

Name____Date__________

Observe and Classify

Suppose you wanted to classify the things you see around you. What kind of a system could you devise?

Pick a spot somewhere on the school grounds. Make a list of everything you see around you.

Think about how the things on your list are alike and different, and how they relate to each other. Plan a way to classify the things on your list. Make a diagram to show your classification system.

Low | Medium | High

Self Assessment

Nombre________________________________Fecha__________

Observa y clasifica

Imagínate que quieres clasificar las cosas que ves a tu alrededor. ¿Qué sistema podrías inventar para clasificarlas?

Escoge un sitio en cualquier lugar de la escuela. Haz una lista de todas las cosas que ves a tu alrededor.

Piensa en qué se parecen y en qué se diferencian las cosas que escribiste en la lista y en cómo están relacionadas entre sí. Haz un plan para clasificar las cosas de tu lista. Luego crea un diagrama que muestre tu sistema de clasificación.

Bajo | Regular | Alto

Evaluación propia

Name____Date__________

Landscaping Plans

What plants would you choose to beautify your school grounds?

Suppose your principal has given you the job of beautifying your school grounds with plants. Do some research about outdoor plants, and pick some plants that would grow well in an area of the school grounds.

Explain in detail why the plants you chose would be well suited to that area.

Self Assessment

Nombre________________________________Fecha__________

Diseños de jardines

¿Qué plantas escogerías para embellecer los alrededores de tu escuela?

Imagínate que el director te ha dado la tarea de embellecer los alrededores de tu escuela con plantas. Investiga acerca de las plantas que crecen al aire libre y escoge algunas que podrían crecer bien en una de las áreas de los alrededores de la escuela.

Explica en detalle por qué crees que las plantas que escogiste son apropiadas para esa área.

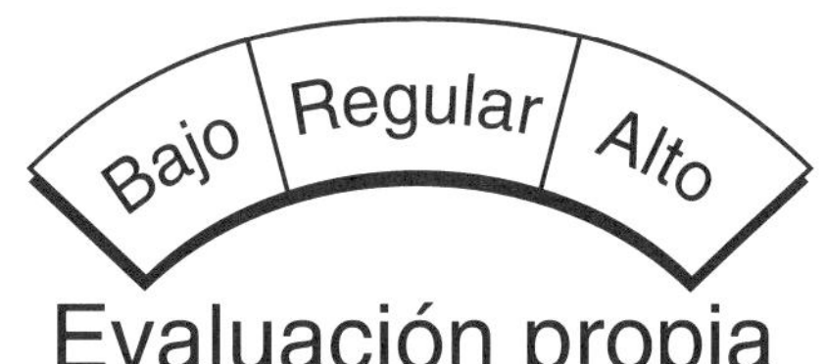

Evaluación propia

Name____Date__________

Paper Bridges

Using just one piece of $8\frac{1}{2}$" × 11" paper, build the strongest bridge you can that will span 7 inches.

Try different designs and test their strength with coins. Tell how you experimented to come up with the strongest bridge. Explain which ideas for strength seemed to work well, and which did not. What makes your design successful? Use diagrams, where helpful, to explain your thinking.

Low | Medium | High

Self Assessment

Nombre________________________________Fecha_________

Puentes de papel

Usando tan sólo un papel de $8\frac{1}{2}$" × 11", construye el puente más resistente que puedas con dimensiones de 7 pulgadas de lado a lado.

Ensaya varios diseños y pónles monedas encima para comprobar la resistencia de cada diseño. Habla acerca de los experimentos que hiciste para poder crear el puente más fuerte. Explica cuáles diseños parecen funcionar bien y cuáles no. ¿Qué hace que un diseño sea exitoso? Usa diagramas donde lo creas necesario para explicar tu razonamiento.

Bajo | Regular | Alto

Evaluación propia

Name______________________________________Date__________

Hanging by a Thread

Make a pendulum that swings at a rate of 60 times per minute.

Make a pendulum with a pencil, a string, and a washer. Explore how you can change the pendulum to increase or decrease its rate. Keep track of every change you make and its effect.

How can you use what you learn from your trials to make your pendulum move at a rate of 60 swings per minute? Tell exactly how to make your final pendulum. A diagram may help.

Low | Medium | High

Self Assessment

Nombre________________________________Fecha__________

Colgando de un cordel

Crea un péndulo que se balancee a una velocidad o rata de 60 veces por minuto.

Crea el péndulo con un lápiz, un cordel y una arandela. Ensaya cómo puedes hacer para que el péndulo aumente o disminuya su movimiento. Anota todos los cambios que hagas y sus respectivos efectos.

¿Cómo puedes usar lo que aprendes de tus ensayos, para hacer que el péndulo se balancee a una rata de 60 veces por minuto? Describe exactamente cómo hacer tu péndulo final. Un diagrama te puede ayudar a hacerlo.

Evaluación propia

Name____Date__________

Ramp Rally

How does the slope of a ramp affect the distance a ball travels beyond the ramp? Find the slope that makes the ball travel farthest.

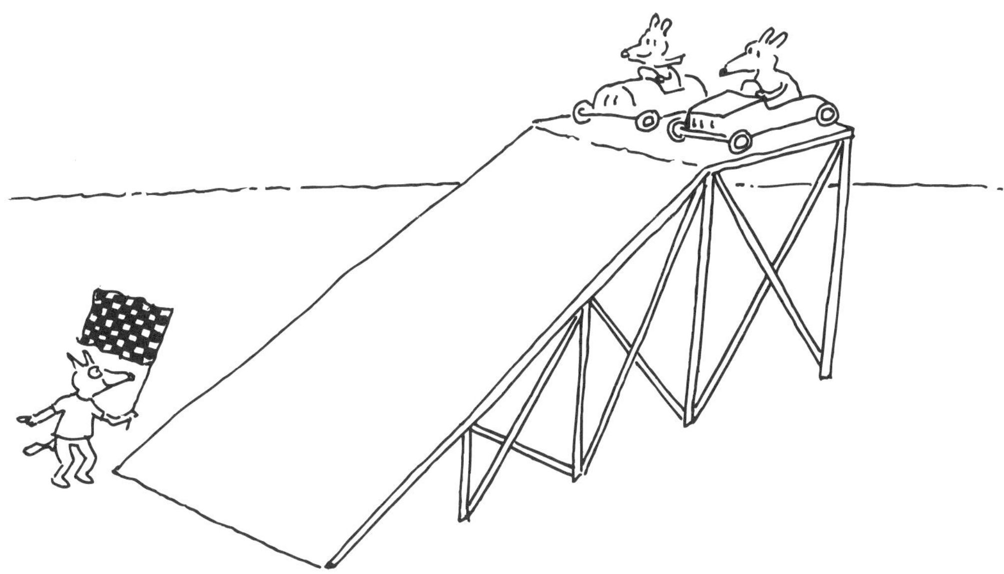

Test different slopes for your ramp. Keep a record of each slope you try and the results you get. Then summarize your findings, and tell which slope is best. You may want to use a chart, table, graph, or diagram.

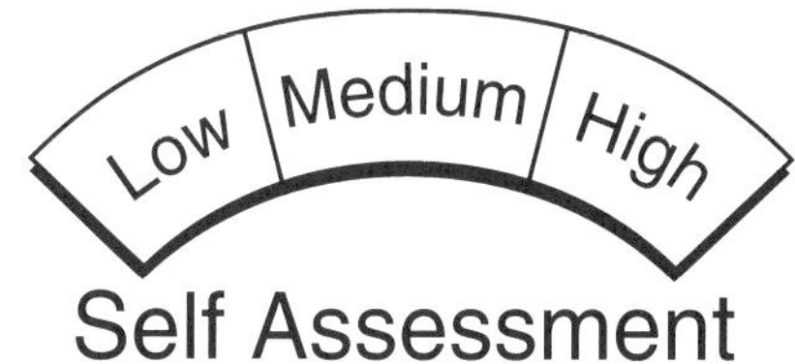

Self Assessment

Nombre________________________________Fecha__________

La rampa veloz

¿Cómo afecta la inclinación de una rampa a la distancia que recorre una pelota más allá de la rampa? Halla la inclinación que hace que la pelota vaya más lejos.

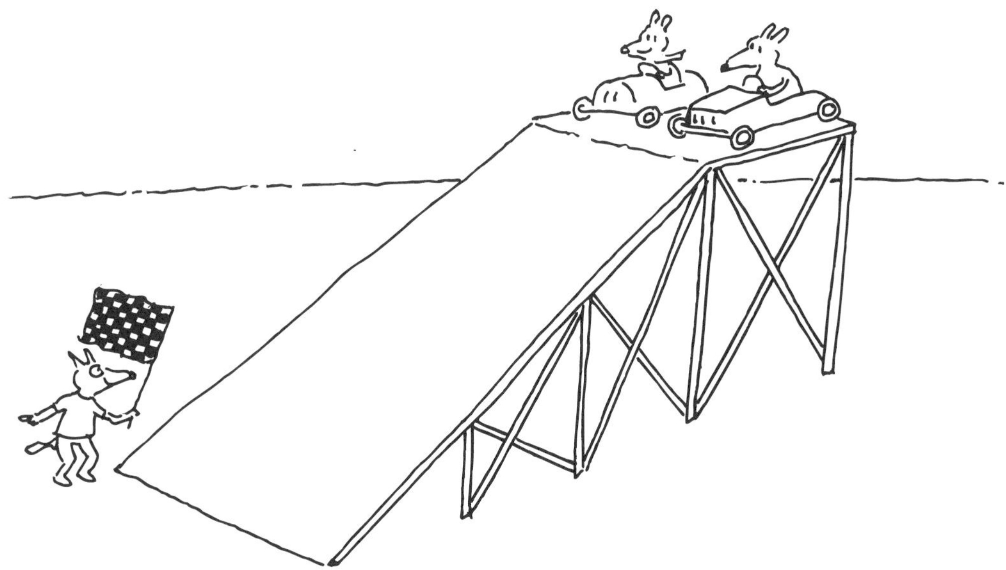

Prueba diferentes inclinaciones para tu rampa. Lleva la cuenta de las inclinaciones que intentes y de los resultados que obtengas. Luego resume tus hallazgos y decide cuál es la mejor inclinación. Si quieres, utiliza una tabla, una gráfica o un diagrama como ayuda.

Evaluación propia

Name____Date________

Ice Insulation

How well do different insulation methods work to keep an ice cube from melting? Design and conduct an experiment to find out.

Think about how you might keep ice cold outside the freezer. Design a fair experiment to test your ideas so that you can learn something about how different ways compare. Plan carefully how you will keep track of the results.

Carry out the experiment.

Write a report describing exactly what you did and what happened. What did you find out?

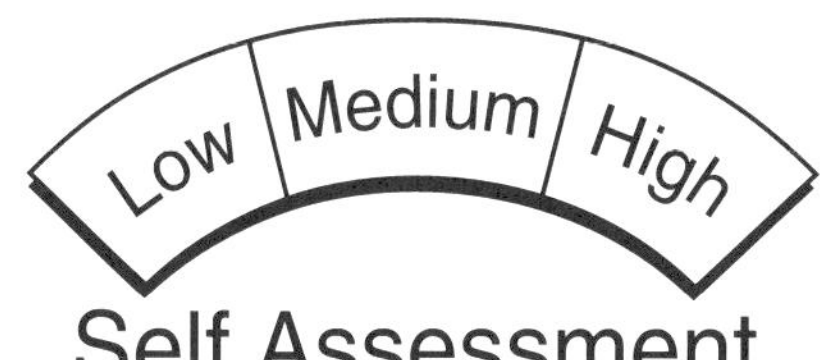

Self Assessment

Nombre_______________________________Fecha_________

Aislemos el hielo

¿Qué tan bien funcionan diferentes métodos de aislamiento, para evitar que un cubo de hielo se derrita? Diseña y lleva a cabo un experimento para averiguarlo.

Piensa en cómo conservar el hielo frío fuera del congelador. Diseña un experimento razonable para comprobar tus ideas y así poder aprender algo acerca de las diferencias entre los métodos. Planea cuidadosamente la manera en que vas a llevar el registro de tus resultados.

Lleva a cabo el experimento.

Luego escribe un informe en el que describas exactamente lo que hiciste y lo que ocurrió. ¿Qué descubriste?

Name________________________________ Date________

Practice Makes Perfect

Think of something that you suspect might improve with practice. Design an experiment to find out if it does improve.

Tell what you want to find out. Think about different ways you could design an experiment to help you find out.

Describe the experiment you think would work best and tell why. Explain exactly how to set up your experiment so that someone else can do it.

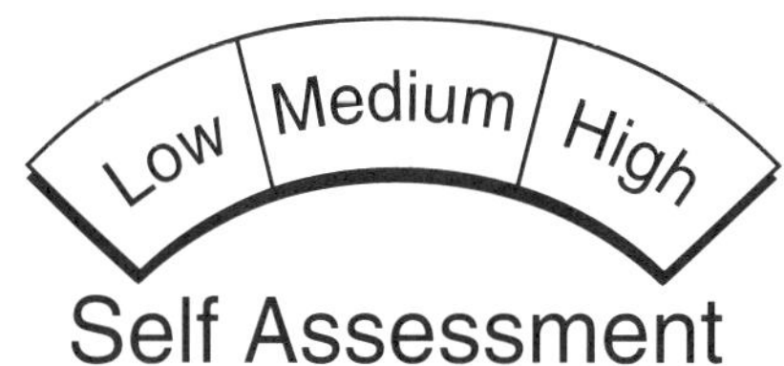

Self Assessment

Nombre________________________________Fecha__________

De la práctica a la perfección

Piensa en algo que creas que se pueda mejorar con la práctica. Diseña un experimento para averiguar si lo que pensaste de veras mejora con la práctica.

Describe lo que quieres averiguar. Piensa en diferentes maneras en que podrías diseñar un experimento para averiguar lo que quieres.

Describe el experimento que crees que funcione mejor y dí por qué lo crees. Luego explica en detalle cómo hacer tu experimento de manera que alguien más lo pueda reproducir.

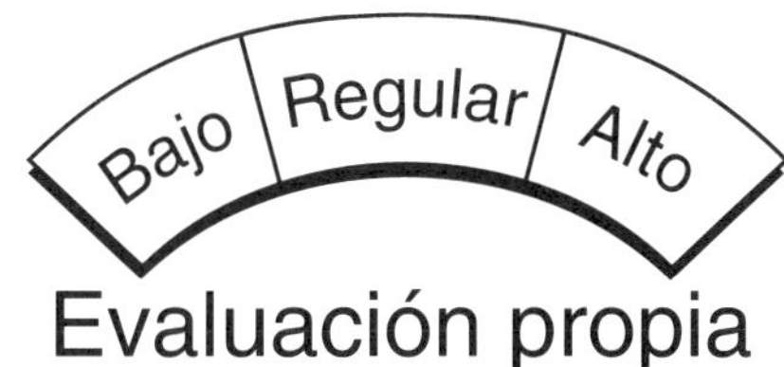

Evaluación propia

Self Assessment

Investigation #____

Name______________________________ Date_________________

How did you do?

Give yourself a score.
Explain your thinking.

Self Assessment

Self Assessment

Investigation #____

Name______________________________ Date_________________

How did you do?

Give yourself a score.
Explain your thinking.

Low Medium High

Self Assessment

©1995 Creative Publications • Puddle Questions™ for Science • Permission is granted to reproduce this page.

Evaluación Propia

Investigación #____

Nombre____________________ Fecha____________

¿Cómo te fue?

Asígnate un puntaje.

Explica por qué te diste ese puntaje.

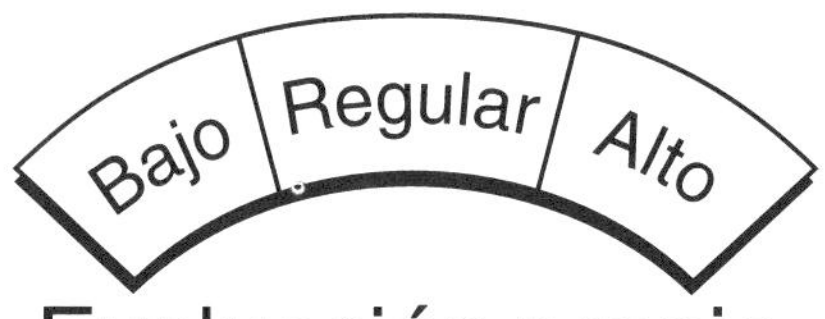

Evaluación propia

Evaluación Propia

Investigación #____

Nombre____________________ Fecha____________

¿Cómo te fue?

Asígnate un puntaje.

Explica por qué te diste ese puntaje.

Evaluación propia

Observation Sheet

Investigation #____

Name______________________________Date_________________

Notes:

Observation Sheet

Investigation #____

Name______________________________Date_________________

Notes:

©1995 Creative Publications • Puddle Questions™ for Science • Permission is granted to reproduce this page.

Record Sheet

Student Names	Date	Investigation 1	2	3	4	5	6	7	8
1.									
2.									
3.									
4.									
5.									
6.									
7.									
8.									
9.									
10.									
11.									
12.									
13.									
14.									
15.									
16.									
17.									
18.									
19.									
20.									
21.									
22.									
23.									
24.									
25.									
26.									
27.									
28.									
29.									
30.									
31.									
32.									
33.									
34.									
35.									